Do-it-yourself
Garden Construction Know-How

Basic research and manuscript
L. Ken Smith, Landscape Architect

Designed by
Craig Bergquist

Special consultants
R. J. De Christoforo
Raymond P. Korbobo, Landscape Architect

Photography by
William Aplin

Illustrations by
Leavitt Dudley

Special projects by
David Geller

Contents

Before you drive a nail

To increase the livability of the space you own—that's the best of reasons for garden fences and walls; garden work centers and storage units; patio floors and overheads; trellises, arbors, and garden gates; windscreens and sunscreens.

Should the patio be expanded for those Sunday afternoon parties? Will a deck at the living room level make the living room look larger? What about a low seat-wall in front of the flower border? Do you need paved paths for the tricycle crowd? Will the vegetable garden function better with a raised bed or two? How about a mowing strip to cut down on hand trimming at lawn's edges? How about a lath shelter for shade while the shade tree grows up?

Think like a pro

When you tackle the job of landscaping a new place or remodeling an old one, you take on the roles of many professionals. You may, temporarily, combine the skills of landscape architect, landscape contractor, engineer, mason, and carpenter.

When your garden development must be very extensive, consider working with a landscape architect or someone similarly qualified when preparing the overall plan. It's also possible to arrange for professional services on a consultation basis.

First things first

Don't be tempted to rush into construction projects or even to plant some trees or establish a lawn without first settling on an overall plan. The impulsive project often becomes a headache or an impediment to other improvements.

Think like a landscape contractor when you schedule your project.

Make a list to establish priorities and to set up a logical order of installation.

Generally, grading, paving and similar basic constructions come first. Do fencing when you're sure access for trucks or tractors, or whatever, is no longer needed. The finishing touches of construction and plantings usually come last.

It's not easy to tear out paving or take down a fence, unless a section of the fence is built so that it can

Brick-on-sand and redwood retaining walls are ideal for do-it-yourself projects.

◁
Brick paving provides a place for outdoor dining furniture. Fencing gives privacy, wrought-iron panel relieves closed-in feeling and allows air circulation.

be easily removed. Garden structures should be viewed as permanent additions. Since they cost something to install and require effort on your part, some pre-planning will eliminate later regrets.

Weather is not as important a consideration for garden building as it is for planting, but relating your schedule to the seasons can help avoid storm damage and ending up working during the worst time of the year.

The plan

Some sort of plan drawn to scale is advisable, no matter who the designer is. Work with graph paper with either 4 or 8 squares per inch, each square to represent one foot. A plan on paper is a record of decisions. In the planning stage it costs nothing to change your mind. Let the plan show the direction of the prevailing wind. How will the plan work with the changing seasons—what protection from the hot summer sun? What about the welcome to the winter sun, low in the southern sky. Mentally walk through the plan. If you find paper plans difficult, stake out the plan on the ground.

Plan on the ground

Regardless of what kind of plan you begin with, and whether or not you're planning a whole new garden or just part of one, a valuable technique is to lay out the overall design on the ground, using stakes or strings. Garden hoses are good for laying out curved forms. Then walk through it, visualizing the various activities that will be taking place. Involve the entire family and get their comments.

You may discover that the children's play area conflicts with what is hoped to be a quiet room. Or that the outdoor living area is planned for the cold, windy side of the house. Eliminate major errors first, then concentrate on the details.

A plan is also the basis for a budgetary estimate. Now is the time to determine how much it will cost to complete the installation, and if the investment makes sense in terms of increased property value and personal satisfaction. From 10 to 20 percent of the cost of house and property is generally considered to be a reasonable landscape allowance. This is usually fully recovered in the sales price should you ever decide to sell.

Is it legal?

When you think like a landscape architect or a landscape contractor, you won't embark upon any building project without first checking out all local planning requirements, restrictions, and local codes. Be sure to verify property lines and to check for easements or right-of-ways. Know where septic tanks (if any) and sewer lines are located. Check your deed for restrictions. Building codes really are established to protect *you*. View the local agency as help rather than hindrance. They know the potential problems and will help you avoid them.

Your neighbors

Cooperate with neighbors, especially on fencing. You must live with them as well as your garden. A view that is great on your side but horrible on theirs is not a way to go.

Area use plan

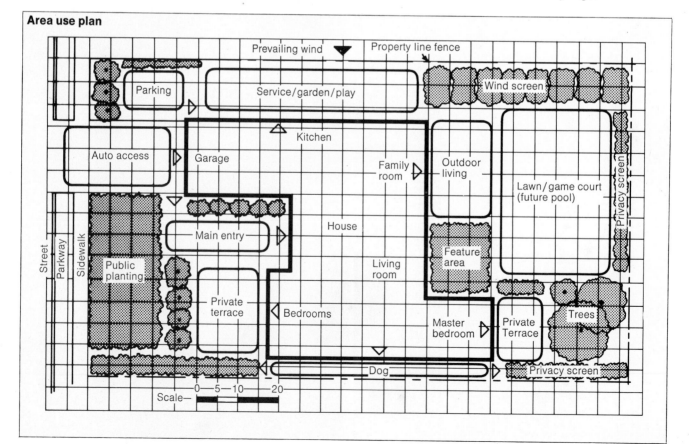

Good site drainage is important for your plants and structures and for your neighbors', as well. Excess water should drain toward the street or into a storm drain. Take all precautions to make sure water does not flow onto adjacent property. Work with neighbors. Often a common drainage ditch will work for adjacent properties.

Remodeling

An existing landscape you wish to change requires a plan of action as much as a new one. Here, of course, you decide what is worth saving or fixing up, and what should be torn out to make the place more suitable for you. Badly cracked paving, and any structurally unsound elements, should be razed. If appearance is your objection, a little ingenuity might lead to a face-lifting to turn an eyesore into a conversation piece—often at a considerable saving.

Builder *and* plantsman

Plants and structures, plants and paving are not enemies. They get along together beautifully. A fence, with vines, may become a vertical garden in one growing season. A deck is a stage for plants in containers. Overhead structures can be designed as vine supports. Many shrubs and trees perform beautifully when trained against a trellis.

Below: Plants blend well with railroad-tie steps, flagstone paving, stone wall, in this garden landscape.

Extensive brick-on-sand patio is laid out between existing trees.

Most garden construction is within the capabilities of the average homeowner.

Bricks laid 8″ wide with mortar joints make a good surface for mower and edger.

Garden floors and decks

Even the most ardent plant lover will concede that some solid surfacing will make a garden more usable. Outdoor living areas, driveways, walks, entry courts, swimming pool decks, atriums, garden work centers and game courts are garden spaces that are usually paved. Actually there need be no conflict between beauty and practicability. Well-designed paving, properly installed, can be a pleasant addition to any garden. Location, size, shape and material are best determined by intended use, along with appropriateness to site, personal preference and cost.

Outdoor living areas, or patios or terraces as they are often called, should be thought of in just that way: areas for living outdoors. People and furniture are as much a consideration as inside the house and they both need some type of flooring. The main difference between indoor and outdoor space is that the scale of an outdoor room can be larger. Areas can be small or large depending on what you wish to accommodate and the square footage you have to work with. Good planning makes maximum use of *any* space.

Too much paving may result in a commercial look. Large expanses can be broken up with plants, or you can use green, wood, or masonry screens to separate areas.

Orientation to sun and wind is of primary importance in selecting the best location. A north or east placement, preferably with a cooling breeze, is best for a hot climate. If you live where every available ray of sunshine is absorbed with delight, south or west will trap the heat, and cold winds should be excluded. Convenience to kitchen or living room, and view and privacy are other factors that may influence placement of an outdoor living area. Don't overlook side yards or the front of the house when there is enough space.

If you are working with a house that faces in the wrong direction you can compensate much with a trellis or shade tree. A removable covering or

Top: Side yard is used for a secluded sitting area. Bottom: Brick-on-sand terrace encircles small pool in this wooded setting.

This outdoor living area uses wood decking, brick-on-sand, and soft paving for a low maintenance garden.

Fences lend privacy to this view deck nestled in the corner of a hillside yard. Landscape Architects, Armstrong and Sharfman.

Dramatic band of paving extends into lawn and embraces tree. Redwood 2"x4"s stained black emphasize design.

a deciduous tree can provide shade in the summer and let the sun warm you in the winter.

Another possible solution, when the situation permits, is to have a second, smaller garden floor or deck with a different exposure than the main one. Then you can decide whether to enjoy the sun or the shade.

Most homeowners inherit their driveways, and unless building a new house, are seldom involved in their design and installation. Often, an existing driveway needs expansion to allow for easy manuevering, turning-

around or additional parking space. Tricycles have a way of turning into teen-agers' cars in a remarkably few years. Sometimes the extra space can serve double-duty as a game court. Since a large area is involved, interest in shape and softening with plants is needed to avoid a parkling lot look.

The best way to lay out an area for a vehicle is to drive it, park it, and turn it around. Mark off the area needed, adding room for walking by when parked; three feet wider than the area needed for the car is a good rule of thumb. Allow plenty of leeway

for trailers, especially if they are to be backed into a parking space. Available space sets the limits on driveway design. But often, even on small lots, there are ways to include offsets for extra parking or turning.

Courts, atriums, garden work centers and other activity areas are also outdoor living areas. They should relate to the interior of the house as well as the rest of the garden. Success results when you do a good amount of pre-planning, bearing in mind the cautions already expressed in regard to traffic patterns, climate, and the like.

Gravel parking space added to existing driveway is inexpensive and avoids harshness of too much solid paving.

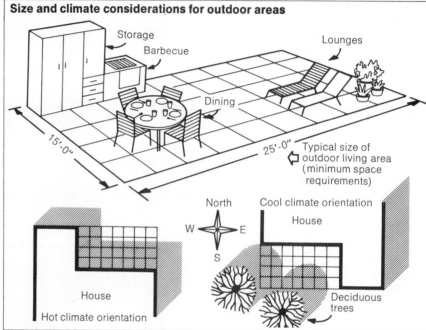

A guide to garden paving

Cost range is for minimum 400 square feet, simple forming, minimal excavation, normal soil and access, all labor and materials by a contractor. Figure roughly one-half for materials only. Prices are constantly changing, usually upward, but relationships between different materials are more stable. Thus if the cost of concrete goes up 10%, brick and flagstone are likely to rise accordingly. This is valuable in making major budget decisions: you can figure that if the top price for a concrete patio is $500.00, brick-on-sand would probably cost $1250.00, and flagstone $2000.00.

Type	Description and Comments	Cost Range per Square Foot
Concrete	Practical, durable, many surface treatments. Cost includes fiber expansion joints.	
Natural	Gray tends to be cold-appearing and glaring. Steel trowel finish is slippery when wet. "Sweat" or "swirl" and broom finishes are non-skid and texture helps break glare.	$.60 to $1.00
Color	Earth tones harmonize with plants. Use others with caution. Integral color mixed throughout concrete is easier than sprinkle-on which can be splotchy.	add 10¢ to 20¢
Salt-Finish	Travertine-like pitted surface derived from rock salt. Coarseness of salt determines the size of the pits. Can be used with colored concrete.	add 10¢ to 15¢
Exposed Aggregate	Pebbly texture goes well with plants and wood, and softens glare. Uneven surface collects dirt and makes furniture wobble. Rounded stones best.	add 50¢ to 75¢
Impressed	Patented process impresses brick, cobblestone and tile patterns into soft concrete. Mortar can be used to fill the joints for a smoother surface.	add $1.00 to $2.00
Light-weight Topping	Troweled-on concrete topping that stays cool, even when in direct sun. Can be textured for added interest.	add 50¢ to 75¢
Fine Aggregate Coating	Franchised method consists of a thin layer of tiny pebbles in an epoxy mix applied over existing concrete.	add $1.00 to $2.00
Acid Stain	Can be applied to new or old concrete, after thoroughly cured. Will not rub off.	25¢ to 50¢

Type	Description and Comments	Cost Range per Square Foot
Latex Coating	Another way to salvage a drab appearing slab of concrete. Tough enough for normal wear.	25¢ to 50¢
Paint	High quality concrete paints hold quite well under proper conditions. Periodic repainting is necessary.	25¢ to 50¢
2" to 6" Sub-base	To minimize cracking in expansive soil or where soil freezes. Cost includes excavation.	add 25¢ to 75¢
Steel Reinforcing	Wire mesh or steel rods as an added protection against cracking where soil conditions are unstable or heavy loads are anticipated.	add 25¢ to 75¢
2x4 Dividers	Permanent strips of redwood or other decay-resistant wood serve as expansion joints and add interest to large areas. Helpful for amateur in setting up grades and levelling concrete when pouring.	50¢ to 75¢ per lineal foot
Vinyl Strips	Attractive expansion joints available in white, black, gray and tan.	50¢ to 75¢ per lineal foot
Brick	Old favorite for garden surfacing. Excellent for homeowner to install. Available in reds, buffs, yellows and other colors. Soft types less expensive, but use harder pavers for heavy traffic and cold winter areas. Cost is for common red brick, laid in a simple pattern.	
Laid on Sand	Easy to do, casual appearance, mistakes or movement easily repaired. Outside edge should be set in mortar or lined with a permanent border. Sweep sand into tight joints.	$1.50 to $2.50
Laid on Concrete	Less subject to movement, can be kept cleaner. Joints are usually mortared. Laying over existing concrete saves cost of a new slab.	$2.50 to $4.00
Used Bricks	Informal effect with rougher surface than new bricks. Joints are usually mortared to fill in irregularities. Inexpensive salvage source can reduce cost.	$2.00 to $3.00
Hot-Mixed Asphaltic Concrete	Best use is for driveways and parking. Because of heavy equipment needed, minimum installation is for 1000 square feet with good access. Cost increases for walks and small areas. Contractor normally includes 2" base with 2" mix over, weed killer and permanent wood borders.	40¢ to 60¢
Seal Coat	Bituminous or epoxy solutions applied over existing asphalt to seal pores and enhance appearance.	15¢ to 25¢
Paint	Must be specifically manufactured for application over asphalt. Follow directions carefully.	15¢ to 25¢
Soil Cement	Mixture of cement and existing granular soil for a casual appearing, reasonably durable surfacing. Good do-it-yourself method.	15¢ to 25¢ materials only
Flagstone	Natural sandstones, granites and slates in ½" to 4" thick slabs. Source of stone determines cost. Thin types excellent for laying over existing concrete.	
Laid on Sand or Soil	Best for natural setting with lawn or groundcover grown in open joints.	$3.00 to $4.00
Laid on Concrete	Better surface for furniture, easier to keep clean, when joints are mortared.	$4.00 to $6.00
Tile	Informal appearing types best for garden use. Available in squares, rectangles and geometric shapes, and several sizes.	
Laid on Sand	Use only strong tiles and make sure base is firm and level, or cracking will occur. Sweep sand into tight joints. Needs a permanent edge to hold in place.	$1.50 to $2.50
Laid on Concrete	Preferred method, with mortar joints. Good material to dress up an existing concrete entrance.	$2.50 to $4.00
Adobe Blocks	Appropriate with southwestern architecture. Laid on a sand base with mortared or planted joints. Availability is limited to certain regions.	$1.50 to $2.50
Pre-Cast Concrete Pavers	Wide choice of colors, sizes, shapes and surfaces. Can be laid on sand base with sand joints or over concrete with mortar joints. Patterned types are good substitute for more expensive clay and stone products.	$1.00 to $3.00
Soft Pavings	Materials that can be walked on and cost less than solid surfaces, yet don't have to be cared for like a lawn or groundcover. A permanent edging of some type is optional. Buying in bulk is much less expensive than sacks.	
Decomposed Granite	Granular material that looks a little like coarse sand. Packs well, and easy to rake leaves off. Usually tan or brown. Good for garden paths, can be used for driveways and parking.	25¢ to 50¢
Brick Dust	Similar to decomposed granite except red.	25¢ to 50¢
Crushed Gravel	Includes roofing gravel of various sizes and colors. Displaces easily and not comfortable to walk on.	25¢ to 50¢
Rounded Stone	¾" mixed stays in place fairly well and is walkable. Brownish tones are attractive, but not always available.	25¢ to 50¢
Bark Products	Looks well and also serves as a mulch for plants. Shredded types form a safety cushion under play equipment. Chips can float away in a rainstorm. Eventually decomposes.	25¢ to 50¢
Pecan and Walnut Shells	Lasts longer than bark. Limited availability.	10¢ to 20¢

Bull-float is used to smooth out concrete. Long handle enables finisher to reach far edge without having to walk on concrete.

A form is constructed to separate paved area into sections. Consider using construction joint between slabs.

Installing garden paving

Let's assume that you've laid out the proposed paved area with stakes and strings as suggested previously, and are satisfied with the location, size and shape. A careful study of the paving material chart and the descriptions that follow can help you decide which paving is best for your specific project. These five basic steps are similar for most of the listed materials:

1. Excavating and Grading—can often be minimized—when local codes permit—by laying the paving directly on top of existing grade. If you want it to be flush with existing grade, or if a sub-base must be used, some soil will have to be removed. To avoid a stepdown from the house, you may want the paving to be at floor elevation (or 1" to 2" below for easy hosing down). If it is to be raised above grade, a sufficient amount of fill will be needed. It must be thoroughly com-

Concrete tamper pushes aggregate down for easier finishing.

Proper ground moisture is necessary for concrete to set and cure evenly.

pacted before any paving is added. Much work can be accomplished with a shovel and a wheelbarrow especially if you have a helpful son or neighbor. You can buy fill and have it trucked in if none is available on your property. Be sure to check local codes to see if fill requirements are specific—if you must buy fill it might as well be the correct material. This is the time to consider over-all drainage. When an area is solidly paved, water can no longer soak in and has to go somewhere else. Be sure there is sufficient pitch for the type of paving selected, and that the water can flow to a street or storm drain without causing damage once it gets off the paving. Use a bubble level on a straight board, a line level, a hand held sight level, or a surveyor's level; don't try to sight by eye—slopes can be very deceiving.

2. Forming—is required for concrete and asphalt and determines the shape, drainage and thickness. The forms are staked and backed with soil so as to be strong enough to withstand the weight of the fluid mass during laying and finishing. Construct concrete forms so they can be easily removable. 2"x4"s with 1"x2" stakes driven on the outside 4' apart are standard. 1"x4"s can be used but require many more stakes. Bender boards (like ½" redwood), hardboard, and plywood are used for curves. For an extra strong edge, deepen the perimeter of the paving with a shovel so that it is thicker than the rest. This acts like a built-in footing.

Asphalt forms are permanent and should be made of decay-resistant

Hand grading

Forming

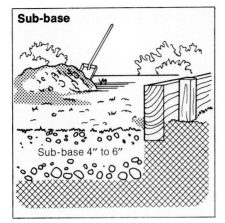

Sub-base

Sub-base 4" to 6"

Sleeves and post anchors

Top: *It's easy to install low-voltage lighting wires through a 2" plastic sleeve laid down before paving. Bottom: To hold a fence or shade structure post, a steel post anchor is secured in concrete footing.*

wood like redwood or cedar or material treated for the purpose. Curves done in wood should be laminated for a minimum 1" thickness. When laminating wood for curves, bend one piece to established stakes first, then bend the second one to mate. Bond them together by nailing through and clinching the nail on the inside of the form. Permanent forms of this type may also be used for brick-on-sand, flagstone, soil cement, tile, pre-cast pavers and soft materials.

3. Sub-Base—is recommended for expansive soils or where freezing and thawing cycles are encountered. Decomposed granite, sand, rock dust, cinders and similar materials are used as a 2" to 6" thick cushion under the paving to prevent cracking, raising or settling. Don't skimp if the need for a sub-base is indicated.

4. Footings, Piping and Sleeves—need to be planned for ahead of time when they occur in paved areas. Building department inspections may be required. Lay out post anchors—for vertical members—and sill bolts—for wooden plates—to have ready for insertion during laying of the paving area.

5. Pre-soaking—soil must be well compacted and uniformly moist before paving material is added. This is especially true for concrete work. Areas that are too wet are as bad as areas that are dry. Work by hand with a garden hose and wet thoroughly and deeply. Do not tolerate pools of water, muddy or soft spots. Dry areas will suck more moisture from concrete than wet areas and it may result in a splotchy finish. Also, be sure to wet down all form material.

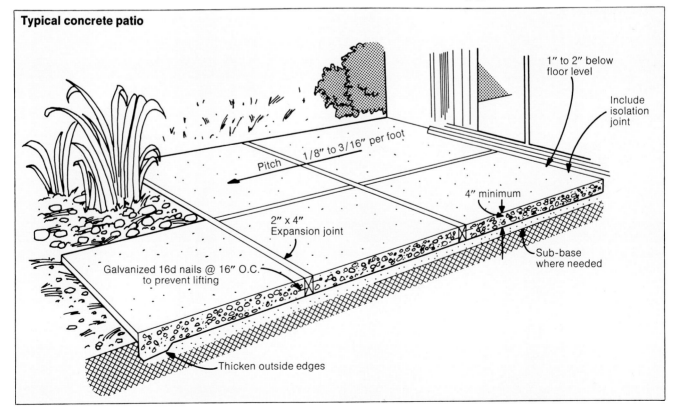

Typical concrete patio

1" to 2" below floor level

Include isolation joint

1/8" to 3/16" per foot

Pitch

4" minimum

2" x 4" Expansion joint

Sub-base where needed

Galvanized 16d nails @ 16" O.C. to prevent lifting

Thicken outside edges

Concrete

Concrete is always practical, but not always appealing. A patio that is a glaring, unbroken expanse of smooth, gray paving is not very interesting. But because there are a great many choices in layout possibilities and in color, texture and patterns, you can have beauty along with practicability.

Concrete work does require some muscle and the thought of a large slab can be a bit frightening, but you can do it if you take a cool approach. Concrete does not set up in minutes and a wet-mix truck is not about to dump a yard on your doorstep and take off. If you visualize the steps to the job and are prepared, you will not fail. Also, there are ways to minimize the work involved. Be the creator, the designer of the project and do all the grading and forming. Then call in commercial people to pour and finish. You will still save a bundle. If you are concerned about a particular finish, buy yourself a sack or two of readymix material and make some stepping stones to practice on before you tackle the big one. Another out is to design a grid-work pour so you can do as many sections at one time as you choose to.

Follow the five basic steps listed above, making sure the forms are secure and that there is a pitch of 1/8" to 3/16" per foot. Then proceed in this order:

1. Control Joints — are needed at crucial points where a crack is likely to occur. A control joint can be cut with a groover to a depth of at least one-fifth of the slab thickness (see illustration). Cracks, then, will usually occur at joints cut with a groover. The idea here is to make them occur where *you* want them to. They should be marked out on the form boards with thumbtacks or some other non-

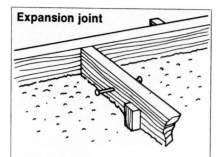

Expansion joint

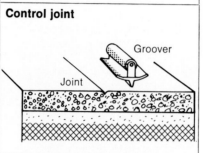

Control joint

Groover

Joint

erasable mark that can be easily located during the finishing process.

Expansion joints serve a similar purpose and should be cut to length and staked into position, except where a truck or wheelbarrow needs to pass during the pouring—or you can bridge over them.

Similar joints—called isolation joints—are used where a new pour abuts a building or existing slabs. Usually, square areas of more than 200 square feet and narrow areas of more than 50 square feet should have some type of expansion control joint. Felt or fiber strips are normally used where appearance is not crucial. In garden situations, more attractive joints can be made with redwood or vinyl strips especially made for that purpose.

2. Reinforcing—is used as a further safeguard against cracking where unstable soil conditions or heavy vehicle loads are expected. Number 10 welded wire mesh in 6"x6" squares, or ½" (#4 bar) reinforcing rod placed at 24" on center two directions with intersections tied with wire is normally used. The reinforcing must be

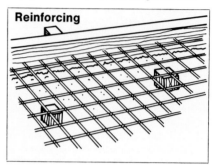

Reinforcing

held up during pouring so that it stays midway in the concrete.

3. Mixing—for small areas requiring one cubic yard or less can be done in a large wheelbarrow or on a flat surface. (One cubic yard covers 80+ square feet placed 3½" deep—the thickness of a 2"x4" form). It's usually wise to order ready-mix concrete delivered to the site in a revolving-drum truck when pouring three or more cubic yards at one time, unless you have a power mixer and a source

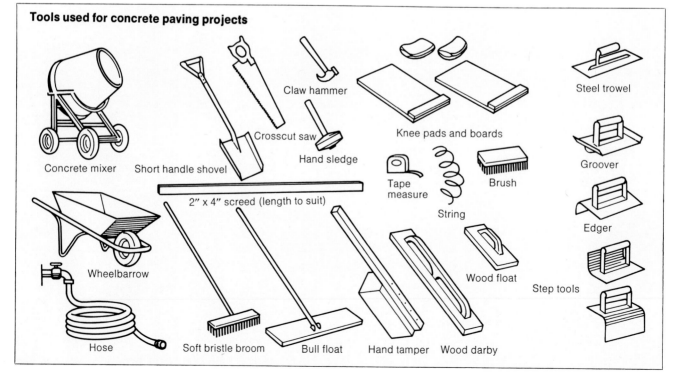

Tools used for concrete paving projects

Concrete mixer

Short handle shovel

Crosscut saw

Claw hammer

Hand sledge

Knee pads and boards

Steel trowel

Wheelbarrow

2" x 4" screed (length to suit)

Tape measure

String

Brush

Groover

Wood float

Edger

Step tools

Hose

Soft bristle broom

Bull float

Hand tamper

Wood darby

Top: Aggregate mixed into concrete, then exposed with broom and water. Center: Wavy broom finish adds interest, increases traction. Bottom: Pitted texture made by sprinkling rock salt on wet concrete.

of willing labor. Also, it is best to estimate the amount needed, then order an extra 5%; too much is better than not enough.

If the truck can't unload directly into the forms, arrange for enough wheelbarrows and strong people to wheel them, or you may end up paying an expensive overtime charge. For difficult access, a pumping machine with a long hose can be rented. Also check mix with local ready-mix—you have several choices with them.

Normal proportions for hand-mixed concrete are 1 part cement to 2½ parts dry sand to 2½ parts crushed rock aggregate (maximum size pieces about ¾ inch), plus 5 gallons of water per sack of cement. (Ready-mixed concrete may use higher proportions for the sand and rock.)

Air-entrained concrete, a fairly recent development, should be used as a protection against freezing/thawing, and de-icing salts. Tiny bubbles of air are dispersed through the concrete and provide relief areas when a freeze causes pressure. Special cement of this type is available, but ready-mix with an air-entraining agent added is better. Check local practice to make certain; mountain areas may require air-entrained concrete even when nearby areas at lower elevations may not. Actually, air-entrained concrete is a good safeguard for exterior work even in minimal freeze areas. Avoid use of salt-finish wherever air-entrained concrete is advisable.

The cost of a 5 cubic yard load of ready-mix delivered to a site within 20 miles of the plant ranges from $100 to $150. (A 3 cubic yard load may cost slightly more per cubic yard.) Materials, including rental of a power mixer would be less than half the cost. But it takes time to round up the cement, sand and crushed rock, and the cement mixer, and a lot of hard work to feed the mixer. Dry-mix aggregates may also be delivered by truck. You add the cement and the water. Packaged mixes are prohibitive in cost for all but the smallest jobs.

Sometimes a suitable stone can be substituted for the crushed rock for use as exposed aggregate, rather than applying it to the surface later on. Availability and cost vary; it's worth checking into as it saves labor and avoids the timing problem of when to add the aggregate.

Mix in a retardant to allow enough finishing time if the weather is hot, or 1% calcium chloride as a quick-set additive if cool and damp. If integral color is to be used, it should be added at the rate of 5 pounds (depending on the color and manufacturer) per sack of cement at time of mixing. Be sure to read the instructions on the package.

4. Pouring—or placing is best done in the early morning. Avoid rainy days, or possible freezing temperatures. Have all tools at hand, and enough qualified help to make sure the surface doesn't set up faster than you can properly finish it. Test the mixture to see that it has the right amount of water content to make it flowable without being too watery and thin. Place concrete as soon as possible after it has been mixed. Pour as close as possible to its destined location. Do not drag or flow the concrete excessively. Work with a square-edged shovel to settle the concrete against the forms but do not overdo. You should avoid pushing all the large aggregates to the bottom of the pour. You must settle them below the surface yes, but that's all. Further smoothing of the surface is accomplished by screeding and finally with a float. Fill the forms and strike off (also called rod or screed) the top by moving a straight 2x4 back and forth across the forms, moving excess concrete ahead of the board, and filling in any low spots behind. Do this as soon as possible before "bleed water" collects on the surface, which will cause dusting or scaling of the concrete surface. Practice varies, but some contractors next tamp the surface a minimum amount with a concrete tamper, wearing rubber boots for areas too wide to reach from the edges. This pushes the aggregate a bit below the surface and makes finishing easier. (Omit the tamping if stone for exposed aggregate has been used throughout the concrete mix.)

5. Finishing—begins as soon as the concrete has been struck off. There should be an absence of water sheen and concrete should sustain foot pressure without damage. "Bull-float" the surface with a wide, long-handled float—relatively simple for small areas, but requiring a delicate touch for long spans. Use a tool called a "darby" for walks and narrow areas (it's kind of a bull-float without the long handle). This helps avoid "dishes" or puddles that hold water. Cut control joints with a groover or jointer. As soon as the surface is firm enough to get on with movable kneeling boards, edge the outside perimeter and along expansion joints, and follow-up by hand floating to smooth the surface (wood floats are commonly used for garden work). If salt-finish is going to be used, sprinkle rock salt on the surface at 5 to 10 lbs. per 100 square feet and tamp in with the wood float.

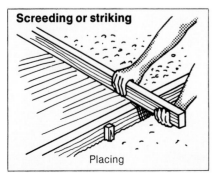

Screeding or striking

Placing

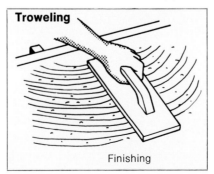

Troweling

Finishing

Exposed aggregate finishes will need rounded aggregate put on with a shovel and tamped and hand floated in similarly to the rock salt, unless it's already in the concrete mix. Angular aggregate can be used, but the surface will be rough and flat pieces tend to dislodge. The secret is not to put it in so soon that it disappears into the concrete, or too late when it can no longer be tamped in.

Methods of finishing exposed aggregate vary considerably. One easy way is to use a soft bristle broom to slightly expose the stones after the surface has set up for a short time. Then when the surface has hardened even further, water is carefully applied and the stones scrubbed clean with the broom or a brush. Applying the water too soon results in loose stones and a very rough surface. Waiting too long can mean not being able to get enough concrete off the stones.

Another way is to hand-set the stones in a pattern. This is a handcraft process and only a small area of 10 square feet or less should be attempted at one time. By setting some of the stones on edge, a very striking effect can be achieved. Best use of this method is for a focal point rather than an entire area.

This is also the time to apply "sprinkle-on" color. Pre-mixed packaged pigment is best and can be used straight from the bag. It should be worked into the surface as evenly as possible with the wood float. (Rate of application varies with color and manufacturer).

A wood float finish is usually too rough except for driveways, ramps and service areas. Final troweling is normally made with a steel trowel as soon as the surface "holds" a finish rather than reverting into a watery mass when troweled. Shuffleboard courts, dance areas and future rooms need a smooth, steel trowel finish, but it becomes slippery when wet and is usually avoided outdoors.

A "sweat" or "swirl" finish is made by a rotary motion of the trowel which gives it a non-skid texture. Power-driven finishing machines make a similar finish and are worth considering renting when laying more than 500 square feet in one day.

By lightly pulling a soft bristle broom over the troweled surface just before it

Curing

has hardened, a neat non-skid surface is created. Texture can be varied by stiffness of the bristle and pressure of the broom and softness of the concrete at time of brooming.

Timing for impressed concrete is crucial. Usually the pattern is pressed in with the special marking device after one pass with the steel trowel. Installation is always by franchised contractors, unless a marking device can be made.

6. Curing—can be accomplished by keeping the slab moist for at least a week. If the weather is extremely hot, building up a sand rim and keeping filled with water will provide protection against cracking. For large slabs, it's easier to do what most concrete contractors do: spray on a colorless

Staining

curing compound immediately after finishing to seal in the moisture. Wait several days before carefully stripping the forms. Keep traffic off the surface to prevent footprints and scratches.

7. Staining—after six weeks or so is another way of coloring an otherwise uninteresting gray slab. If the concrete has evenly cured with no obvious dark spots left, and the surface is clean, applying acid stain according to the manufacturer's directions is usually highly successful. A heavier, follow-up coat that evens up the color is also available. (Curing compounds affect penetration of the stain and should be omitted if staining is planned.) This is also an excellent method to use on existing concrete, provided it's in good condition with no structural defects, and any grease is thoroughly removed with tri-sodium phosphate.

Quaint brick paving can be duplicated with an impressed pattern in colored concrete.

Staining redwood expansion joints makes them an integral part of the color coordination.

Much patience was required to create this beautiful surface of hand set stones. The cost is nominal if done by homeowner.

Brick

On a letter grade basis, brick would probably rate A+ as a garden paving. It's non-skid and non-glare, comes in colors and sizes that are just right for garden use, can be laid in a variety of patterns and combinations, and is ideal for do-it-yourself projects.

The best way to select color and type of brick is to look at what choices are offered at local brick or supply yards. Then order enough to complete the job, figuring 5 normal-sized bricks per square foot to allow for some breakage; common bricks are approximately 3¾" wide x 2¼" thick x 8" long. This will guarantee that you won't end up having to buy more later that don't match.

Bricks are heavy and you can't haul very many at a time in the back end of a car. They usually come in palettes, and are often delivered in multiples of 500, which should be placed as near as possible to the work area.

Pattern can be decided upon by laying out bricks in different ways to see what looks and works best. Running bond is simple and well adapted to brick-on-sand. Basketweave leaves a large joint at one end, so is better with mortar joints. Stacked bond or jack-on-jack can look crooked and is difficult for large areas. Herringbone

requires lots of cutting if the edges are to be straight. Variations are infinite, but simplicity is usually better than complex patterns which appear busy and are more difficult to lay.

Decide if the bricks will be laid on sand or on a concrete base. Check thickness and size of the specific brick selected. Complete the five basic steps, paying particular attention to grading the sub-base as smooth as possible. Unless subsurface drainage is extremely good allow 3/16 to ¼" per foot pitch, and then proceed as follows:

1. Sand Base — 1" ± (plus or minus) deep, needs to be firm and level or bricks will end up tilting all directions. In mountain and other severe winter climates, the sand base must be 4" deep and should also extend 4" beyond the outside row. This will minimize heaving caused by the expansion of frozen soil. A special screed made by notching a straight 2"x4", or with "ears" nailed on can be used to scrape a setting bed of sand to exactly the right depth. The bricks should be ¼"+ above the adjacent edge when first laid, which allows for tamping and settling. A rubber mallet or a short length of 2"x4" laid over the bricks and tapped with a regular claw hammer will set the bricks with a

Herringbone

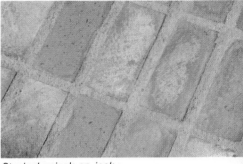

Stacked or jack-on-jack

Running bond

Combination Curved

Basketweave (above and below)

This circular terrace looks difficult to build, but it's simply a matter of laying one brick at a time; corrections are easy to make. Pictured at right are some popular paving patterns.

A specially notched board, or screed, is used to scrape setting bed of sand to even depth.

To avoid breakage, a short length of 2"x4" is tapped with hammer to set bricks into place.

The type of pattern chosen will determine the amount of special cutting needed at edge of paving.

minimum of breakage. Tight joints (⅛"± wide) are usually used and filled by sweeping in sand. Bricks can also be set ½" to ¾" apart and then filled with either a dry mortar mix and carefully wet with a hose, or with wet mortar squeezed from a grout bag or poured from a container with a spout. Finish the joints flush and smooth with a joint tool or, as a substitute, a short length of ¾" pipe which will make a concave joint. Used brick, because of its irregularities, cannot be set closely enough together for tight, sand joints and is better spaced out for mortar.

When using mortar joints, a 2" sand base mixed dry with 2 sacks of cement

Spreading sand and then sweeping it into place is best with tight joints of ⅛" or less.

2"x4" makes a suitable permanent edging to hold brick-on-sand firmly in place.

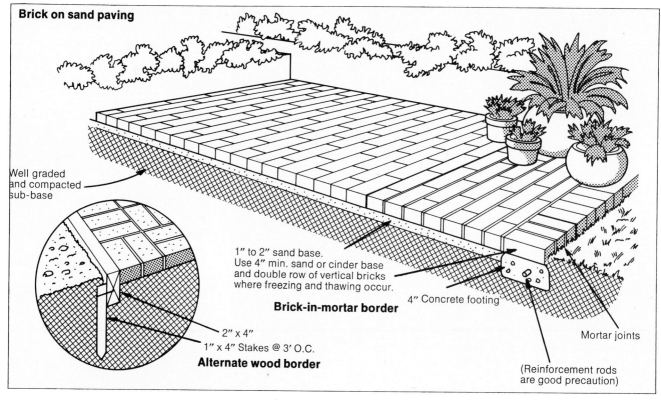

Brick on sand paving

Well graded and compacted sub-base

2" x 4"
1" x 4" Stakes @ 3' O.C.
Alternate wood border

1" to 2" sand base.
Use 4" min. sand or cinder base and double row of vertical bricks where freezing and thawing occur.
Brick-in-mortar border

4" Concrete footing

Mortar joints

(Reinforcement rods are good precaution)

Finished project incorporates railing and built-in bench. Landscape Architect, Jack M. Smith

per 100 square feet can be used in areas not subject to deep frost. Spray lightly after laying bricks until thoroughly wet. Wait at least 24 hours to fill in mortar joints.

A natural look can be achieved by filling the joints with a soil mix and growing grass or groundcover between the bricks.

Try to avoid cutting bricks by laying them out for full size wherever possible. Some cutting is unavoidable.

How neatly it is done is often the difference between a good job and a poor one. Soft bricks can be cut with a brick set, by giving it a sharp blow with a hammer. Hard bricks are more difficult to cut because they shatter easily. Water lubricated masonry saws slice through bricks as if they were butter. You may want to look into renting one or marking all bricks and taking them down to the brick yard to be cut at one time (charges usually vary

from 5 to 10 cents per cut).

Brick-on-sand needs a permanent border to hold the bricks in place. One method is to set the outside row on edge or on end for a deeper edge.

Another way is to lay the outside edge on a concrete or mortar base with mortar joints. An easier way is to install an edging of treated or decay-resistant wood such as redwood 2"x4"s, or railroad ties. Concrete is also suitable.

Tools used for brick paving projects

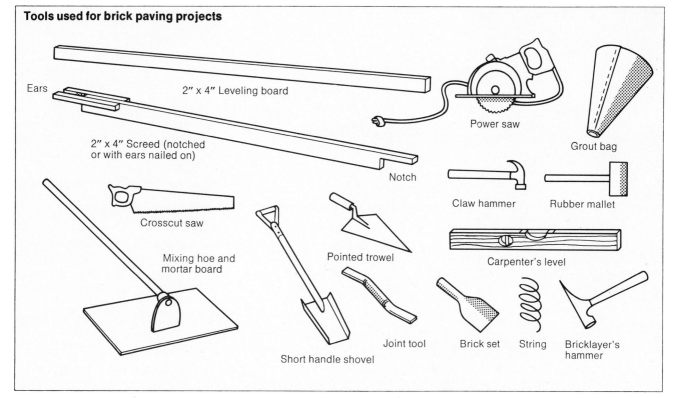

Ears

2" x 4" Leveling board

Power saw

Grout bag

2" x 4" Screed (notched or with ears nailed on)

Notch

Claw hammer

Rubber mallet

Crosscut saw

Mixing hoe and mortar board

Pointed trowel

Carpenter's level

Joint tool

Brick set

String

Bricklayer's hammer

Short handle shovel

A mortar base is best for keeping bricks firm and evenly spaced.

Color is added to mortar mix for subtle blending of bricks and joints.

Trowel handle is handy for tapping bricks into place.

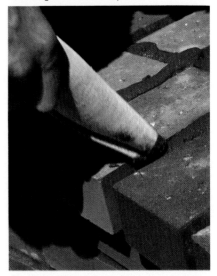

Similar to decorating a cake, a grout bag is used to squeeze wet mortar evenly into joints.

Soft bricks do not shatter easily and can be cut with a brick set and hammer.

2. Concrete Base — can be a new 3″ slab or an existing piece of concrete. Be sure to allow for thickness of brick and ¾″ mortar setting bed. Once you get the hang of it, it's fairly simple to squish the brick lightly into the setting bed and level it with a long board reaching from one edge to the other. The bricks should be wet down with a hose before laying, for a better bond. Check spacing (pieces of plywood are good spacers) and level before filling in the joints with mortar. Bricks can also be laid on sand over the concrete, as described above.

Mortar Mix — is composed of 1 part cement to 3½ parts sharp sand plus ½ part fireclay or lime. Omit the fireclay or lime if plastic cement is used. Mix dry materials thoroughly first and then add as much water as you need to bring the mix to a plastic, workable state until mortar is a buttery consistency. Color is often added to the mortar for paving to help the joints blend in with the bricks. Packaged mixes are expensive, but convenient. They're fine for small jobs where the extra cost would be minimal.

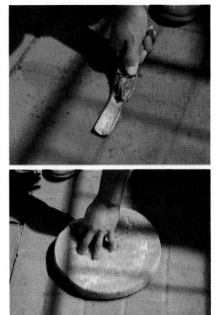

Top: Joints are firmed and shaped. Bottom: Large sponge is used for cleaning bricks. An acid wash of 20 parts water to 1 part muriatic acid can be used after mortar has cured.

Aggregate shows slightly, but is firmly held in place, for an interesting asphalt surface.

Fine sand is used to fill small cracks prior to applying seal coat.

Applying a seal coat over asphalt will enhance appearance and protect surface. Any repairs and cleaning should be taken care of first.

Asphalt

Asphalt is much maligned as a garden paving, often unfairly. Asphalt costs less, blends nicely with the adjacent street and is less inclined to show grease spots. It is also a good material for storage areas, walks and game courts. However, its use for outdoor living areas is limited. Appearance is just not as attractive as many other types of paving. Furniture can sink into the surface if softened by the sun. Unless painted, the natural dark color absorbs heat, making it uncomfortably warm in the summer.

Hot-mixed asphaltic concrete is a miserable material to work with. It takes a big truck to deliver it, and is best when finished with a heavy roller. Cold, plant-mix asphalt is easier to handle, but has the major disadvantage of taking months to reach full hardness. Doing the subgrading and forming yourself, and having a contractor do the rest is a possibility, especially if adding on to existing asphalt. Even here, the sub-base should be rolled with a heavy roller or power compactor, equipment that would have to be rented.

Be sure to get a specification from the contractor and see that he follows the five basic steps. Check forms to see that there is a minimum pitch of 1/4" per foot.

There are two special surface treatments that might be considered. Sprinkling cement over a newly-laid asphalt surface and wetting with a fine spray will make a harder surface. It's very difficult to apply evenly, and the finished result is almost always a blotchy gray. However, it may be worth doing if a seal coat or asphalt paint is planned anyway.

Gravel chips are sometimes rolled into asphalt before the surface has hardened. The chips tend to work loose unless the asphalt is still soft enough when applied; light colors give a speckled appearance that detracts more than enhances. Dark chips can look nice if the timing of the application was just right.

Patching small areas of existing asphalt *is* something that can be done without special skills or equipment. Packaged mixes that only require the addition of water are available and can be used to fill in the cracks, broken edges and settled areas.

It's also easy to apply a seal coat over existing asphalt to hide patches and seal the surface to make it cleaner and better looking. Thoroughly clean the surface, fill small cracks with fine sand, then apply evenly with a large brush or "squeegee." There are various products readily available for filling cracks, sealing and filling as coating.

Painting asphalt can both seal the surface and enhance the appearance. It should be in good condition, or imperfections will show even more than if left unpainted. Light colors will show grease spots if used on driveways and parking areas.

Soil cement

This little-known paving is relatively inexpensive and requires no special skill to install. The existing soil *must* be sandy, or granular like decomposed granite; fine particled clay soils won't combine with the cement satisfactorily.

Informal driveways, parking areas and walks can be paved with this method making use of existing soil. If you want the advantages of a solid paving at a low cost, with the appearance of hard-packed soil, this may be the answer. The surface is somewhat dusty, so don't expect it to sweep as clean as regular concrete. Chances are you won't be able to find an example to look at, so make a small test area first to see if you like the results, and how your soil reacts with the cement. Give the test area all the rough treatment it might get under ordinary use. If it's paving for a driveway, try a spot where you can drive a car over it.

Installation is as follows:

1. Grade the overall area with a slope of 1/4" per foot. Install permanent forms at edges if a neat border is desired.

2. Install piping or sleeves if needed.

3. Rototill to a 4" depth and rake out until free of rocks, plant growth and debris.

4. Spread cement as evenly as possible at the rate of 4 to 5 sacks per 100 square feet.

5. Thoroughly mix the cement with the soil to a 4" depth with the rototiller.

6. Drag smooth and compact with a heavy lawn roller. Repeat several times, fill in low spots, and drag again to remove all footprints. A simple drag can be made from a 4 foot long 2" x 4" with added weight on top. Raking tends to leave small depressions.

7. Wet down with a fine spray and repeat until saturated.

8. Roll again as soon as dry enough to work without sticking or leaving footprints.

9. Keep traffic off and spray lightly for several days until hardened.

Flagstone

Natural stone paving can vary from sophisticated slate set in a precise rectangular pattern with matching color mortar joints, to rugged sandstone set irregularly directly in the soil with creeping plants growing in the cracks. There are enough types and ways of laying flagstones to fit any garden and preference.

Cost is practically the only limitation. If you're lucky enough to live near an inexpensive source of stone, this may be an excellent paving material for you. Or, you may use a small amount of stone in combination with a less expensive material to limit costs

Some of the softer stones can be cut fairly easily with a brick set. Harder ones may require careful chipping or cutting with a masonry-blade saw. Obviously, it's best to try to work with the natural shape and size as much as possible and do as little cutting as necessary.

Here are several ways to lay flagstones. Complete the five basic steps where applicable and then begin:

1. Sand Base — needs to be slightly deeper than for brick, 2″ in mild climates to 6″ where winters are severe, to allow for the irregularities of the stone. Stones laid on sand should be 2″ or thicker to prevent cracking. Screed the sand off

similarly to when laying brick, then move the flagstone around a little with both hands to seat it in the sand rather than relying too much on tapping into place. Since it is difficult to make the joints tight enough to fill with sand, use either topsoil and plants, or mortar. Permanent forms or edging are optional but a good idea.

2. Concrete Base — is similar to that described for brick paving. Lay a few flags at a time in a ¾″ mortar setting bed, leveling with a long, straight 2″x4″ and leaving the joints open until the job is complete and you're satisfied with the pattern. Keep mortar off the stones as you work; it's hard work to get it off after it sets. Take care not to crack stones while working. Stones as thin as ½″ will be strong enough after the mortar sets.

3. Soil Base — can be used for a casual appearance where a little irregularity is acceptable. If an existing lawn isn't working very well as an outdoor living area, lay out the stones right on the lawn, and score around them with a shovel. Set them aside one-by-one, and dig out a resting place directly in the soil. Dip deep enough so you can use sand as a sub-base. This will allow you to seat the flags firmly to eliminate rocking and cracking. The result is a flagstone terrace with lawn already growing in the joints. To save digging, and if you want to raise the area anyway, remove existing plant growth, lay on top of the existing grade and fill the spaces between with a soft paving material, or with topsoil if you want to grow lawn or groundcover.

Tile

Precision-made tiles can appear too refined and artificial unless used in close association with architecture and structure. They are an excellent indoor-outdoor paving for entrances and garden rooms.

There is, however, a wide variety of informal-appearing tiles that are more at home in the garden itself. They range in size from 4″ x 4″ to 12″ x 12″ squares and also come in rectangular and other geometric shapes. They are available up to 2″ thick, with a textured surface, and in colors including grays, yellows, browns, and reds. Once you've decided that this is the effect you want, and the cost falls within your total landscape budget, select the specific tile from the assortment available.

Flagstone is a versatile, natural paving that fits almost any garden. It can be moved and re-used if not set in mortar.

Decorative tiles can be chosen from an assortment of shapes and colors.

Apply the five basic preparation steps, allowing for a minimum pitch of ⅛″ per foot for drainage. Grading and sub-base preparation should be as accurate as possible. Cutting is best done with a masonry-blade saw, so layout for full pieces is desirable.

1. Sand Base — is only valid for strong tiles that won't crack with normal use. A common procedure is to place sheet plastic or heavy roofing felt over a sand bed. This helps achieve levelness and prevents weeds or grass from coming up through the joints. The idea is especially good when the pavers are butted or a sand joint is used. Installation is basically the same as for brick, except a level setting bed and neat placement is even more critical. Using a 2″ to 4″ sand base mixed with cement as described for brick provides a stronger base and minimizes cracking of the tiles. Tight joints can be swept with sand, or wider joints can be filled with mortar.

2. Concrete Base — is preferred for tile work. Again, follow the instructions for brick.

Adobe blocks

If you have a house in the "mission" or "Mediterranean" style, here is a paving you can lay yourself, that will truly harmonize. Generally available in California and the Southwest, adobe bricks are sturdy enough for this use, being manufactured with an asphaltic stabilizer, not simply made of mud and straw. However, they are still subject to wear from heavy use, and even if protected with masonry sealer, they tend to have a "dusty" look.

As with used bricks, adobe blocks are irregular enough to make a tight joint impossible, and should be spaced 1 inch apart for mortar or topsoil. Installation is similar to that for bricks except allow for the different size (8″ wide x 16″ long x 4″ thick), and make sure the setting bed is firm and level, or the blocks will be subject to cracking.

Pre-cast concrete pavers can be laid singly, or set in sections to form a pattern.

Pre-cast concrete pavers

If laying concrete is a task you'd rather avoid, you can use pre-cast concrete pavers instead. Unless you decide to make the forms and manufacture them yourself (which is not difficult if you have plenty of time in which to pour and cure enough of them), the cost will be considerably higher. The advantages are that you don't have to worry about how the finish will turn out, and you can lay them one piece at a time, at your own pace.

Choice goes way beyond the old, gray 12″ square stepping stone. Sizes up to 30″; squares, circles, rectangles and hexagons; many colors; and exposed aggregate, wrinkled ,and other surfaces are available. Some even look like tile, brick and cobblestone.

Installation is similar to laying brick and tile, with the same choices for type of base and joints. Some can even be laid directly on top of a lawn or dirt area as a temporary patio. Cutting is best with a portable circular saw and masonry blade, so limit cuts as much as possible and avoid small pieces.

Soft pavings

Some garden situations call for a surfacing other than lawn or groundcover that costs less than solid pavings and is softer appearing. Other common requirements are that it can be walked on after being wet, that it doesn't readily wash away, can be kept free of weeds, doesn't get spread all over the neighborhood, and isn't too dusty.

Generally, a material for soft paving use should have a range of particle sizes that will pack together and therefore stay in place better than one with all one particle size.

Picture a walk made of marbles and it's easy to see why certain gravels and stones move around so much when you walk on them.

It should also be reasonably free of soil to eliminate mud and dust and

allow it to dry quickly. Also, the more soil-like it is, the more weeds that will grow in it. Tar paper or plastic laid underneath retards weed growth, but also affects drainage and often shows if the material gets displaced. It's easier to pull out the weeds since they're usually weak anyway, or use chemicals to control.

Grade the area to be covered so that it has a minimum slope of ¼″ per foot, and take care not to block water and create a miniature lake.

1. Decomposed or Disintegrated Granite — is a granular material containing both fine and coarse particles. Usually tan, brown or gray, it not only satisfies the requirements listed above, but is also pleasant to look at. Frequently used for driveways and walks, it should be placed 2″ to 4″ deep, wet down, and tamped or rolled until firm. An occasional raking, and pulling or spraying weeds is all the care it needs. It can be installed with a permanent border, which is a good idea, or just blended into the surrounding soil. Keep away from house entries; it scratches floors if tracked in. Will erode if much water runs across it or if slope is too great.

2. Brick Dust — is similar to decomposed granite, except it is reddish in color.

3. Crushed Gravel — comes in small, ¼″ sizes to the common concrete aggregate size of ¾″ and larger. Hard to walk on, especially in bare feet, it doesn't pack very well (keep out of parkways and other public areas). Many colors are available, depending on source rock—some are even painted. Whites (usually quartz) show every leaf or bit of dirt; bright colors look artificial. Lay 2″± deep and contain with a permanent edge slightly higher than the gravel to reduce scattering.

4. Rounded Stone — can be obtained from pea gravel (¼″±) size up to 2″ and larger diameters. ¾″ mixed stays in place fairly well and is walkable. It serves nicely in side yards and garden work areas. Some tan and gray colors are quite attractive and falling leaves blend in rather than stand out Usually installed 2″ to 3″ deep with a permanent border. "Mud-aggregate" can be made by tamping stones into muddy soil so that when it dries they stay in place better.

5. Bark Products — are natural appearing and work well as garden paths and under play equipment.

Soft pavings of rock-in-soil, decomposed granite and bark chips are applied for a natural effect. They are best suited to level areas with good drainage.

New bark should be added as the old decomposes; a continuing process. If it decomposes to where it no longer serves as a paving, use it as a mulch or soil amendment and replace with new. Should be laid 2″ to 4″ deep depending on the coarseness and use. Shredded bark usually stays in place fairly well, but large bark chips sometimes float away in a rainstorm, so avoid use where water is apt to flow.

This entry walk is made of 2" x 4"s nailed to stringers resting directly on ground.

Log cuts have a natural character all their own.

Wood sections set on end are the "bricks" for this paving. Note longer sections serving as retaining wall and steps.

Wood

There are two basic ways to use wood as a garden flooring: in the ground as a paving, and above grade as a deck. Either way, it's a warm, handsome material, having a quality all its own, and very much at home in the garden.

Being subject to deterioration and damage by dry-rot and insect attacks, it's crucial to select the correct type of wood, preservative treatment and construction technique. If this is done,

it can be as permanent as many other paving materials. Wood used as outdoor flooring also needs to resist warping, checking and cracking, be reasonably free of splinters, and be strong enough to withstand the loads and type of wear that it will receive. Rougher textures are usually best for both appearance and safety; smooth surfaces such as finished planks and log cuts sometimes become slippery when wet.

In the ground

This is advisable only for those types of wood that are naturally resistant or have been treated to withstand below-grade conditions. Heart redwood (solid red color with no light streaks of sapwood) will last for many years with no additional treatment. Most heart cedar, cypress and seasoned black locust are similarly resistant.

Common construction lumber such as Douglas fir and pine must be pressure-treated if it is to come in contact with soil (pressure-treated lumber, in all dimensions, is now available). Brushing on, or even soaking in a preservative may be of temporary value, but it seldom penetrates far enough into the wood to allow it to be used below grade.

Termites are a problem in all but a few states so wood laid in the ground should not touch house walls. Otherwise, a direct path is created for the insects, and it could result in structural damage to wood house parts.

Pressure-treated railroad ties (or timbers where ties are not available) are excellent for use as garden paving. Lay directly in the ground or on a sand base with the 8″ side on top for maximum coverage. Select pieces with fairly square edges to avoid large cracks that could cause tripping, or space several inches apart for lawn or groundcover. (See *Recycled and Inexpensive Materials* for more information.)

Log cuts 3″± thick are cross-sections through the trunk of a tree. Dig out a space, loosen the soil at the bottom and drop into place. Being 12″ to 36″ in diameter, they leave large spaces between, which can be filled with lawn or groundcover, or a soft paving. Mixing the sizes reduces the spaces. Don't use in an area where they won't be continually moist, as they tend to crack from drying out.

Wood blocks 6″± long, cut from the end of a 4″x4″, 6″x6″, 8″x8″, 6″x8″, etc., be set on end on a sand base. Prepare the base similarly as for bricks (except deeper) and put them tightly against each other to avoid wobbling. This is a good way to use short pieces of lumber that are often thrown away.

Other treated or decay-resistant wood pieces can be laid directly in the ground or on a sand base as long as they are at least 3½″ deep (a 2″x4″ laid with the 2″ dimension on top is okay, but not if laid flat), and nailed together to prevent lifting and warping. This becomes quite expensive unless you have a source of scrap lumber, or are working with a small area.

Another method is to dig out an area 6″ ± deep, lay 2″x4″ or 4″x4″ stringers directly on the ground and then nail a wood surface such as 2″x4″s on top. Sunk flush with the grade, it will appear to be wood paving. Such pieces can be pre-assembled as grids and then placed. Be sure to provide a way for water to get out from under.

All wood must be decay resistant or pressure treated. A 2″ sand base makes laying easier. (Illustration at right.)

These redwood 4″x6″s are laid on a sand base and nailed together through the sides so that no nails are visible.

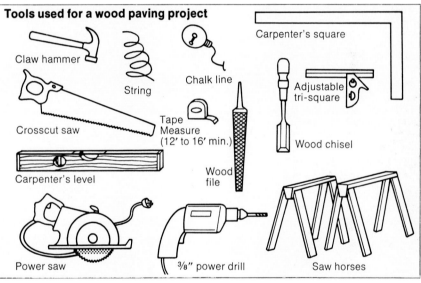

Tools used for a wood paving project

Claw hammer

String

Chalk line

Carpenter's square

Crosscut saw

Tape Measure (12′ to 16′ min.)

Adjustable tri-square

Wood file

Wood chisel

Carpenter's level

Power saw

⅜″ power drill

Saw horses

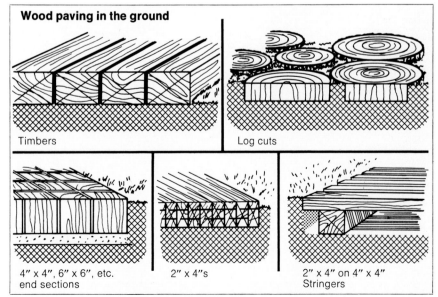

Wood paving in the ground

Timbers

Log cuts

4″ x 4″, 6″ x 6″, etc. end sections

2″ x 4″s

2″ x 4″ on 4″ x 4″ Stringers

This deck was built in less than an hour. The inside planks are left unnailed for easy dismantling and storage.

stringers should be treated or be decay-resistant, but the planking will last a long time even if it isn't. Brushing or pouring preservative on the stringers and the bottom side of the planks may help slow down deterioration.

A variation is to lay the stringers on a base of crushed rock or raise them free of the soil on bricks or concrete blocks. This will prolong the life of the wood, especially if the space underneath is kept dry and free of leaves and debris.

Raising the stringers (girders) up higher on a masonry footing so that there is a minimum of 6″ clearance from the ground will provide even further protection. Pre-cast concrete piers set on footings are sufficient for most low decks. Footings for cold

Decks

All decks are within the range of anyone who can use a hammer and a saw. Snow loads on raised decks are a factor in northern and mountain climates and they must be designed for. Building permits are usually required. Some building departments consider a wood deck to be the same as an interior floor and insist on an 18″ crawl space below. Always grade the area below the deck so that the water drains away.

A major advantage of wood decks is that they can be built up to the level of the house, or extend space over a slope without having to fill in solidly below. In some cases it costs no more

to build such a wood deck, than it would to construct a retaining wall, import fill, and pour a concrete slab.

A wood landing outside a door can soften the transition from the house elevation down to a lower grade if it isn't practical or desirable to raise the entire outdoor living area. Extended along the house, it becomes a handy ledge for container plants, washing windows or sitting on.

A simple technique is to lay 2″x4″ or 4″x4″ stringers right on existing grade and nail planks to top. This is a good temporary construction that can be dismantled for winter storage or moved to a different location. The

An easy-to-do wood deck serves as a patio and an attractive transition from house to lower grade.

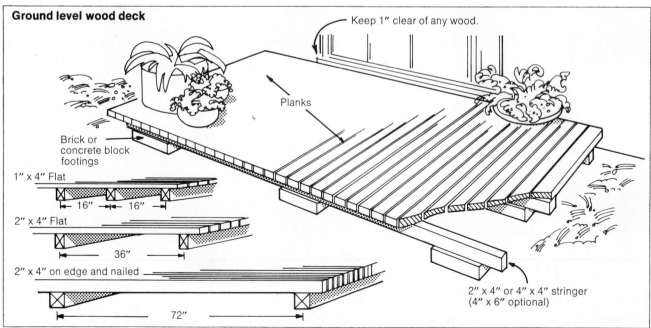

Ground level wood deck

Keep 1″ clear of any wood.

Planks

Brick or concrete block footings

1″ x 4″ Flat
16″ 16″

2″ x 4″ Flat
36″

2″ x 4″ on edge and nailed
72″

2″ x 4″ or 4″ x 4″ stringer
(4″ x 6″ optional)

Left: Height of this deck was determined by view when sitting down. Built and designed by the owner; total material cost of $250.00. See illustration below. Right: Deck is raised up to floor level for easy access from house. Steel supports form railing posts.

winter regions must be below frost lines (up to 36″ deep); footings should be individually designed for hillside decks. Termite shields between the footing and the girder can also be included.

Planking can be 1″x4″s spanning 16″ from joist to joist, 2″x4″s laid on edge spanning up to 6′ if nailed together, or 2″x4″s to 2″x12″s laid flat and spanning 3′± and up to 4′ for full, rough 2″x12″s. Choice depends on scale, appropriateness to site, personal preference and cost. 1″x4″s are actually only slightly cheaper than 2″ thick planking since the joists need to be closer together and more nailing is involved. Diagonal or parquet or mixed patterns can be used, but a 90° side-by-side layout is easiest to install and

doesn't look busy. When placing planks, try to put the natural "cupping" down at the edges to minimize curling.

Start with a small crack (the thickness of a 16d nail is a handy spacer) when laying planking flat. This will allow for the inevitable shrinkage that will occur and makes for easier drainage and cleaning. 2″x4″s laid on edge will not shrink significantly and can be held apart with ¼″ thick spacer boards at 24″ intervals. Stagger splices for strength and appearance. (See page 94 for nailing.)

Girders and joists and shear (diagonal) bracing should be calculated by a structural engineer for large or hillside decks. Often, the local building inspector can provide

specs. For small, low level decks, common sense and rule-of-thumb can be used, allowing a large safety margin. The extra material is usually less than the cost for structural calculations.

Girder spans are generally estimated as being the same number of feet as the depth of a 4″ member is in inches. Thus, a 4″x6″ would span 6′, a 4″x10″ would span 10′. Joist spans vary proportionately to their spacing—the farther apart the more deck load they carry. It's generally safe to span 6′ with a 2″x6″ joist, 8′ with a 2″x8″ etc. when spaced up to 36″ on center. If 4″ wide joists are used, a slightly wider distance can be spanned. Always consult local codes when in doubt.

Criss-cross 1″x4″s nailed from post

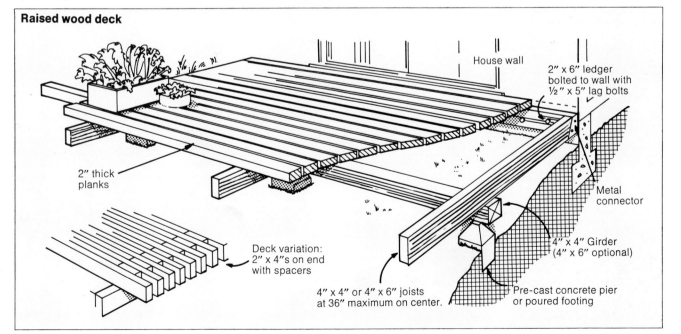

Raised wood deck

House wall

2″ x 6″ ledger bolted to wall with ½″ x 5″ lag bolts

2″ thick planks

Metal connector

4″ x 4″ Girder (4″ x 6″ optional)

Deck variation: 2″ x 4″s on end with spacers

4″ x 4″ or 4″ x 6″ joists at 36″ maximum on center.

Pre-cast concrete pier or poured footing

Rooftops can offer excellent outdoor living space, as with this deck built on a flat-roofed garage.

Hillside deck under construction shows supporting framework.

The Sonotube cardboard forming is a convenient way to pour deck piers.

to post are necessary to prevent cross sway. A good test is to try to move the deck back-and-forth by pushing on an outside corner. If there is much movement, bracing should be added.

Railings

The higher up a deck goes, the more likelihood that steps and railings will be needed. A 12" high deck should have at least one place with a step for safe and easy access. When 18" is reached, a railing, bench or planter should be considered to offer protection from accidentally falling off the edge. Most building departments require a 30" to 36" high railing for decks 48" or higher.

Steps can be built of wood or masonry. (See chapter on *Walks, Steps and Ramps.*)

Railings are a little trickier. Standard wood construction is to bolt minimum size 2"x4" uprights to the joists with two ½" diameter carriage bolts to give rigidity (two uprights at each joist looks better). A 2"x4" top rail, middle and bottom stringer will span 6'± between uprights. Common variations include: omission of the middle stringer and spacing 2"x2" uprights 6"± apart between posts; a 2"x4" laid flat on top of the 2"x4" rail for resting elbows; a 2"x6" instead of a 2"x4" for the top rail. If privacy is needed, solid panels of plywood, fence siding, plastic or canvas can be used.

Wrought-iron can also be used for railings for maximum view. Unless you have welding skills and equipment work with the pre-fabricated units that are available from nation-wide stores.

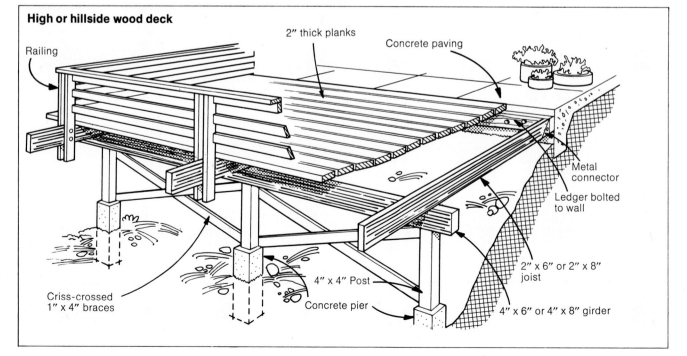

High or hillside wood deck

Railing

2" thick planks

Concrete paving

Metal connector

Ledger bolted to wall

2" x 6" or 2" x 8" joist

Criss-crossed 1" x 4" braces

4" x 4" Post

Concrete pier

4" x 6" or 4" x 8" girder

Limited depth for paving was a problem so full-sized bricks were cut and layed over existing slab.

Even with as little as ¼″ there are still several choices. Products consisting of a fine pebbly aggregate in an epoxy base can be trowelled on. They are usually marketed under a trade name and applied by a franchised contractor. Latex concrete coverings that are troweled on in a similar manner are also available. And don't overlook outdoor carpeting and artificial turf.

Asphalt surfaces that are too far gone to paint or seal coat, can be renewed by laying 1″ of hot-mix asphaltic concrete with a finer aggregate than used for original work. Taper out at edges or replace the existing border to accommodate the added depth.

If possible, design deck railings to match style of architecture.

Adding on

Unfortunately, it's not always just a matter of installing a new piece of paving. Often, it's already there; and it may not be satisfactory. Existing pads installed with a house are often too small to serve as a patio or terrace. Rather than tear it all out and start over, consider adding-on or laying over it. A secret to successful adding-on, when the original material can't be closely matched, is to use a contrasting color or material.

Sometimes the solution is quite simple. If a concrete area has an acceptable surface free from structural cracks, and it drains well, applying acid stain as previously described may be all it needs. If there is enough depth to add another paving on top, it's obviously advantageous not to have to remove and haul away the old slab. Special epoxy cements are avail-

able for adding thin layers. Adding concrete, brick or flagstones requires 3″± for the extra thickness. For smooth surfaces, roughen up the old paving by chipping with a masonry hammer, pick or cold chisel for a better bond with the covering. Painting the surface with concrete glue will also help.

Wood can also be laid directly on a concrete slab with special mastic. Or wood "sleepers," which are usually 2″x4″s, can be attached with concrete nails, expansion bolts or in mastic, and the planking nailed into the sleepers.

When there is less than 3″ to work with, split brick, tile, pre-cast concrete pavers or ½″ thick slate can still be added. In fact, with these materials, the ¾″ mortar setting bed can be omitted, and a thin layer of special mastic used instead.

Exposed aggregate complements existing concrete to increase paved area.

1.

2.

3.

4.

5.

Walks, paths, ramps, steps

Many garden walkways are too narrow. Single-file walks can be 30″ wide, but 36″ is better. Entry walks for two persons side-by-side should be 48″ to 60″. When a walk is adjacent to a wall or fence, some extra width will avoid scraped shoulders.

It's okay for the walkway-width to vary. Actually, it provides more interest than a monotonous ribbon. Gentle curves, subtle changes in direction, function as well as a direct route, and make for a prettier landscape.

A gracious and inviting front entrance sets the mood of a house. It should be safe, and good to look at. Since the driveway often serves as an entrance walk, you can add a parallel strip of paving so it will be easier to get by parked cars. Street parking will be more convenient if you provide landings at the curb. When lot size permits, incorporate a separate walk to the front door. A generous landing at the door is always better than a small stoop. It then becomes a nicer area for greeting guests or for seeing them off.

Since the square footage involved is usually relatively small, the front walk is where a more expensive paving might be used. Brick, flagstone and concrete with a special non-skid surface treatment are good choices. Sometimes the landing can be raised up to floor level with one or two steps, and an indoor-outdoor material such as slate or tile extended from the entry hall for a truly elegant effect.

Traffic patterns should tie together various areas of the garden. The system should be complete—no missing links! List all the various routes needed, and when possible, physically try them.

Practical considerations come first. How do guests get from the curb to the front door? Will it be convenient to carry groceries from the car to the kitchen? Is there a paved surface—preferably without steps—for trash barrels, lawn mower and the like? Does the system consider play areas, a dog run, a route for the mailperson, and so on!

◁

1. Redwood timber path blends with planting. 2. Concrete sculpture adds drama to wood entry pads. 3. Existing narrow concrete walk is widened with exposed aggregate bands. 4. Curbside landing reduces maintenance. 5. Railroad tie and brick steps widen driveway.

24″ Too narrow

36″ or more Better

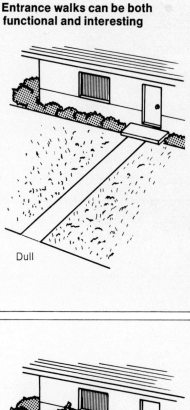

Entrance walks can be both functional and interesting

Dull

Interesting

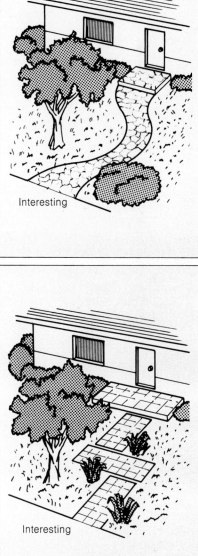

Interesting

29

Tile risers enrich these well-constructed brick steps. Design, Kirk Aiken

Notched 2"x12" stringers with planks for treads are simple to build.

Careful forming is required for overhanging concrete steps such as these.

Existing concrete steps were enhanced by imaginative addition of wood facing and decorative posts.

Considerable skill was required to build this brick ramp.

Service walks can be paved at less cost with plain concrete, soil cement or asphalt. The main requirement is practicability, unless it happens to be visible from an important window or outdoor area. Often, a service walk can be widened or soft paving added so it can serve as a work or storage area as well. This is a good solution for the area between garage and property line that may be too small for other uses.

The garden path should invite a stroll through your private landscape. Groups of narrow trees can be planted in even a small yard. The path may meander behind shrubs or on a slope; it can direct one to a view area, a special planting or to a hidden play-house. Brick, wood and soft pavings like decomposed granite and bark are great for this use.

Ramps

Gardens that are not flat call for ramps and steps to get from one level to another. Ramps are convenient for portable barbecues, lawn mowers and other wheeled equipment, and they are safer than steps for elderly persons and those using crutches and wheelchairs.

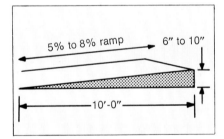

A rise of 5 to 8 percent is a gentle and comfortable slope. This works out to a rise in grade of 6 to 10 inches for each 10 feet of horizontal distance. A rise of 12 inches in 10 feet, or 10 percent, is considered the maximum allowable steepness for a walk. Steps are desirable when the slope is more than 10 percent and, of course, when a ramp is not feasible. A combination step-ramp can be the solution to an existing situation.

Steps

Safety is a major consideration in the design of ramps and steps. The paving must be non-skid. Risers less than 4 inches high and tapered risers where the height varies should be avoided. Also, it's wise to plan for all risers and treads in one flight of steps to be the same.

The relationship of riser to tread can be more flexible outdoors than in a building where space is limited. Concrete steps are usually formed

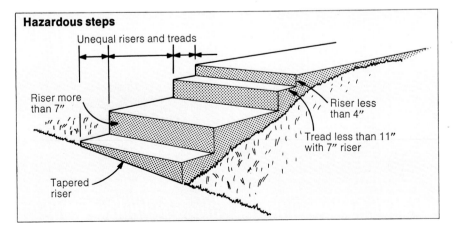

with 2"x6" board which gives a 5½" riser. The tread should be at least 12 inches wide; 16 inches is recommended. If there's room for a smaller riser of 4 to 5 inches, the tread should be widened to 17 to 19 inches. The general rule is—wider treads go with lower risers. This makes for more walkable steps and proportions that are more pleasing and more in scale with the outdoors. Consider 7 inches as a maximum for the riser. Treads should not be less than 11 inches with a 7 inch riser.

Major steps leading to outdoor living areas should be wide enough to permit ease of passage and to relate to the scale of the total area. Think in terms of 8 feet or wider, and consider ends that "run free," or about large pads, built-in planter boxes, and the like.

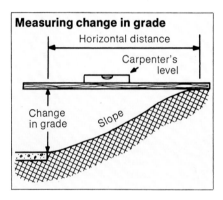

Measuring change in grade

Horizontal distance

Carpenter's level

Change in grade

Slope

Steps require careful planning and layout. One elevation, such as the city sidewalk, is almost always a fixed starting point. The steepness of grade, and the elevation at the other end can be altered by regrading. Often, you can work with safe and attractive riser-tread relations simply by moving some soil or digging into a bank. If both ends of the proposed stairway are fixed elevations, keep a proper riser-tread relationship by making the stairway longer than you might otherwise.

To determine the best riser-tread relationship, lay a straight 2"x4" at the top of the slope, level it with a carpenter's level placed on top, and measure down to determine the total change in grade. Measure the horizontal distance and record both on a piece of graph paper, using a 1 inch square to represent 1 foot. Sketch in different combinations that might do and select one that is appropriate for the material to be used. Include a quarter-inch per foot wash (cross slope) for tread-drainage.

If a slope is too steep for the maximum acceptable 7 inch riser x 11 inch tread, you can set the steps at an angle to the slope or incorporate landings or both.

Adapting steps to a given slope

6" risers and 18" treads

¼" per foot wash

Existing slope

1. Railroad ties are ready-made for garden steps. 2. These granite steps will last forever. 3. Hillside steps of log cuts fit sloping terrain.

Step layout

Top of slope

Down

Toe of slope

Too steep
7 risers

Top of slope

Down

Down

Landing

Landing

Toe of slope

Toe of slope

Angled
8 risers

Jogged
9 risers

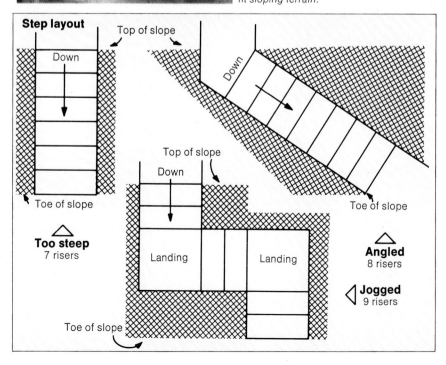

Wood steps

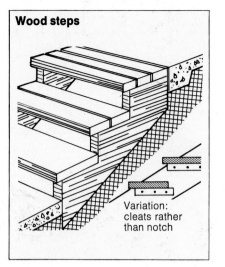

1. Wood Plank — steps with wood stringers are popular since they don't require a large footing, and can be designed bridge-like over terminal supports. Rough 2″x12″s (decay-resistant or treated) can be notched to receive the treads, or cleats can be nailed or bolted to the wood for step supports. Temporary (or permanent) 2″x4″ stakes will hold stringers in place during assembly. Actually, the project may be assembled as a unit and then set into place. This is often more convenient than on-location work.

Railroad tie steps

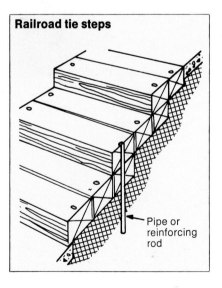

2. Railroad Ties — are stable when set on compacted soil. Select ties with good edges and use the 6 inch dimension as the riser. The simplest way to secure the ties is to drill a 1″ diameter hole 12 inches from the end of each tie and drive a ½″ steel pipe or a ¾″ reinforcing rod into firm ground. Galvanized nails (20 penny) or larger can be used to connect the ties to each other. Provide a 4″ coarse sand base and drive pipes to below frost depths in cold regions.

Concrete steps

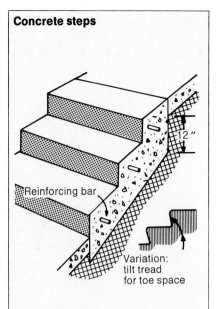

3. Concrete — is the old standby for steps. Forming is a little tricky; the boards for the riser faces and edges have to be stripped so that the exposed portion can be finished. This means that the stakes should be driven outside the concrete; fairly easy to figure out for 2 or 3 steps, but more difficult for long flights. Try to find an example by a professional to use as a guide.

Brick steps

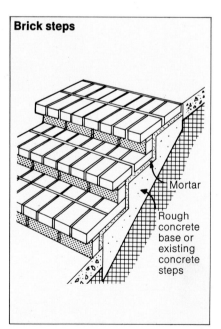

4. Brick, Tile, Flagstone and Pre-Cast Concrete Pavers — can be laid over a rough concrete base, or over an old set of concrete steps if the top and bottom landings can be made to work out. Lay out modular materials like brick before pouring the base to make sure the risers and treads fit without requiring excessive cutting.

Ramp steps and log cut steps

5. Concrete Blocks, Heavy Log Cuts, Thick Flagstones — and similar materials can be set directly in the soil when conditions permit. Don't work this way unless the slope is gentle and the soil stable. They can do the job when set carefully so there is no rocking. They must not tilt out of the ground when walked upon. When you are in doubt, play safe and set such materials on good concrete footings, or a sub-base of stable sand or gravel.

Combination steps

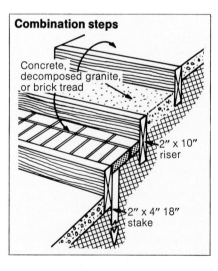

6. Combinations — of several materials are frequently used for garden steps. Brick-on-sand can be placed behind a rough 2″x6″ riser nailed to 2″x12″ stringers, or 2″x10″ risers securely staked with 2″x4″s, long enough to be firmly embedded. A railroad tie riser can be back-filled with decomposed granite or brick dust as the tread surface.

Check local codes to find out if railings are required. Usually, codes are mainly concerned with stairs connected to a structure. Often railings are omitted from garden steps with five or less risers, unless they are exceptionally steep. You can make some personal judgments in these areas. Being safe is better than being sorry or being sued. Even low stairways should have a railing if they will be used by handicapped or elderly persons. Widening a set of narrow steps can often eliminate the need for a railing. This approach probably will look better and may cost less.

Unless falling through is a factor (children, pets), stair railings are usually a top rail placed 30 to 34 inches above the nose of the treads. A simple wood railing consists of 4"x4" posts (decay resistant or treated lumber) set 24 inches deep in concrete, at 6 foot maximum on center, along the edge of the steps, capped with a surfaced 2"x4" nailed flat to the top of the posts and extending 6" past the end posts. Edges should be rounded and sanded, and sealed with an exterior stain to eliminate slivers.

Variations include: decorative posts which you can turn on a lathe; or a second 2"x4" nailed 12 inches above the treads for added strength; or solid sheathing of exterior plywood or fence siding; or the use of nylon rope, iron chain, or the like as railings.

Railings of standard pipe and plumbing fittings are another alternative. Although extremely functional, they are far from handsome and look out of place in a garden setting. Some craftspeople make such materials more handsome by working them over with wire brushes, filing fittings so they blend into pipe, and using black paint for a wrought iron look. Others combine pipe with specially made wooden fittings or use pipe in conjunction with conventional wooden posts.

Wrought-iron railings are a good choice since they can be added to concrete or other masonry steps by drilling post-holes in the concrete and setting the posts with quick-set cement compound. Flanges are available for most post designs so attachment can be done by drilling holes in concrete for masonry fasteners and using lag screws to fasten. They can be installed at the edge of the steps in similar fashions. Ready-made wrought iron railings are generally available. Sizing to suit the project doesn't require more than cuts with a hacksaw. Often, the fence sections are designed so they can be slanted to suit a slope or the rise of steps.

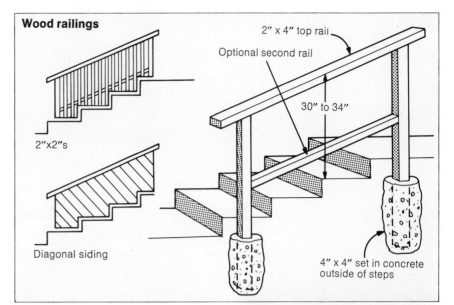

Wood railings

2" x 4" top rail

Optional second rail

2"x2"s

Diagonal siding

30" to 34"

4" x 4" set in concrete outside of steps

Sturdy wood railing is firmly bolted to supporting members.

Chain strung between wood posts is simple railing for little-used steps.

Wrought-iron railing is set within concrete steps, could also be added later at edge of concrete.

Wood construction is appropriate choice for this railing.

What could be more fitting than white picket fences for these historic Williamsburg houses?

Fences and walls

Don't rush to enclose a property. It's too easy to overlook important factors in relation to the design, material and type of construction that is best for a particular situation. The quickie solution often solves one problem at the expense of another.

First, consider the purpose of the fence. Protection of property, security for pets and children, privacy, are usually the prime requisites. But, partial screening, separation of use areas, sound barriers and climate control are also possible objectives.

Welcome breezes should be permitted to enter the garden, strong winds excluded. A 6' fence at the property line may have little effect on the wind reaching an outdoor living area twenty feet away. A fence with air spaces for the wind to filter through may tame it better than a solid one where the wind is likely to swirl over the top and back down again.

If a strong, prevailing wind makes an outdoor living area uncomfortable much of the time, a high, solid wall to deflect the wind, may be effective if placed immediately adjacent to the area. Glass or clear plastic can be used if an opaque sheathing will exclude a view.

Objectionable views can be screened out by proper placement of a fence of sufficient height. Desirable views can be saved—even "picture-framed" by lowering fence-height or using see-through construction.

The reason for a fence may vary from one part of the garden to the next. So different types may be in order. Be sure there is good reason for a fence. Many properties can make use of shrubs and trees to separate areas. The point is—greenery can function as fencing or minimize its need.

Fencing should be an attractive addition to the garden. Usually, a fence is best treated as simple background for planting rather than being too detailed in itself. Detail, however, is acceptable when the project is a major design factor in the landscape plan.

Appropriateness to site and structure is very important. A plastic fence might be entirely compatible with very modern architecture, but grapestakes or rough rails might be more fitting for a ranch-style house. A fence will usually be more harmonious

Good design can turn a slope problem into an attractive landscape feature.

Plastered concrete block wall, tile roof and white chimney blend harmoniously.

Grapestake fencing ties in with texture and color of shake roof.

when it repeats some color or texture or material of the house.

Another aesthetic consideration is whether the fence should be level, slope, or jog to conform to the topography. The tranquillity of a garden scene is disturbed when a slightly "crooked" background serves as a reference point. A typical exception is a rustic fence that rambles with the contours of the land.

Maintenance is an important factor. It can be a mistake to base a selection solely on cost. Nothing can make a property look more run down than a fence that sags and warps and requires bracing. Materials that need frequent painting can become a burden and a continuing expense over the years.

A fence affects neighbors, so reach agreements before starting to build. Discover any difference of opinion right off. A compromise can be great

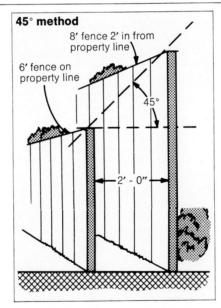

45° method

8' fence 2' in from property line

6' fence on property line

45°

2' - 0"

especially if it leads to splitting costs and having the fence straddle the property line. Also, a fence that looks

well from either side demonstrates more quality and consideration than a "one-sided" type.

Verify property lines and check deed restrictions and local building codes for height and other requirements. Normally, fences or walls within the front yard setback are limited to 42"; others no higher than six feet. This affords enough privacy in most situations. If a higher fence is desired, a 45° upward angle starting 6' high at the property line, and sloping upward is one method used by many agencies to determine allowable height. Thus, an 8' fence can often be built if set in 2' from the property line.

If a swimming pool or other construction requiring heavy equipment is planned, build fences that will allow access, and that will conform to pool fencing laws with no or minimum changes.

Sound and privacy

Security

Wind

Installing fences and walls

Studying completed projects is one way to get ideas for your own. Study the fence and wall chart; read the installation directions that follow, before making a decision.

Use stakes and string to lay the fence out exactly as it will be installed. You can preview the finished project by hanging newspapers over the string to determine the angle of sight from various locations.

Wood

A wood fence is one of the most popular landscape construction projects for the do-it-yourselfer. Equipment needs are minimal and the project doesn't have to be built in a day.

Start with the basic frame of 4"x4" posts and 2"x4" top and bottom stringers. Choose the panel material from the long list of types and sizes of wood. Consider the endless variations that are possible, and it becomes apparent that there's a wood fence to satisfy almost any requirement.

Design should allow for normal weathering without looking shabby. Textured surfaces, stained instead of painted, hold up well outdoors. Wood that is sturdy and nailed securely to minimize twisting, warping and cracking will continue to look good for many years with little care.

Wood posts buried in the ground are subject to rotting out at soil level; how long it takes depends on the type of wood, soil, climate and other factors. Wood in contact with the ground (or on concrete footings) should always be heartwood of a decay-resistant species such as redwood, cedar or cypress, or be pressure-treated.

Common practice is to accept the fact that some posts will eventually have to be replaced or reinforced. Other choices such as steel pipe posts cost considerably more, and post anchors imbedded in concrete don't afford sufficient vertical support.

Constructing the basic wood frame

1. Use stakes and string to establish the fence line. Divide the distance between corner posts into equal spaces not to exceed a maximum of 8' each, unless using pre-cut stringers (see number 3). Dig the post holes to allow for a minimum 24" of post in the ground for fences 4' to 6' high, 18" for 4' high or less.

A clam shell digger or hand auger will work well in most soils, but you can rent a power auger if you want

Pretending that newspapers on a string are the top of a fence helps determine height needed for privacy from neighbor's sliding doors.

the job to be easier and go faster. The two-man type is safest and less apt to throw you when catching on a root or a rock. A heavy, steel digging bar can be handy if you encounter a rock.

It's not a good idea to dig post holes with a shovel. The intent should be to form a 6" diameter hole with minimum disturbance of adjacent soil. This is tough to accomplish with a shovel; holes will be too large and will require excessive amounts of concrete or backfill. The backfill is not an availability problem but over-wide holes will reduce post stability.

2. 4"x4" posts are strong enough for normal fence loads. Free-standing end posts with no return, and posts for small gates can be made stronger by digging deeper holes and using longer posts. (Corner posts of wood

fences are braced by the framing from two directions and normally need no additional support.)

Strengthen posts for heavy gates with diagonal bracing to the next post, or use a 6"x6" instead of a 4"x4", and set it 3' deep.

Set corner posts first, using a carpenter's level on two adjacent surfaces to make sure they're plumb. Temporary braces driven into the ground and nailed to the posts will keep them straight. Stretch a taut line between the top corners of the posts. The string will sag if the run is more than 50'. But you can set an intermediate post as a height guide.

Set other posts along the line established by the string. Posts can be cut to length as you install them or you can saw them off later.

Nailing the boards to the frame is a satisfying finale to the previous work.

Heavy steel angle on a concrete footing offers firm support and holds wood clear of soil.

Middle rail adds strength to this 7' high fence.

4"x4" posts extend 6" above top of fence to support a 2"x6" cap. Vine will climb into open space to show from both sides.

Posts are usually set in concrete, especially where there is a wind load on a solid fence. The concrete can be mixed by hand, since the amount needed is relatively small (See chapter on *Garden Floors and Decks*). Extending the concrete slightly above grade and tapering it away from the post is good practice. If the soil is stable, and the winds not expected to be severe, the post holes can be back filled with well-tamped soil or gravel. Low fences or rail types are often done this way. Don't move posts until the concrete has set. Hold off on framing for at least 24 hours.

3. Install stringers with galvanized or aluminum nails. The upper stringer is often placed flat on top of the posts, and secured with two 16d nails. Cut the bottom stringer to fit between posts. Attach by toenailing

with two 8d nails. Toenailing will be easier if you nail a temporary 2"x4" block below the stringer to provide support.

There are other methods of attaching stringers—some provide more strength, others contribute to appearance. Dadoes, mortise-tenons, and the like will be easier to do if you cut them before setting the posts. Do layout work very carefully when you work this way.

This also applies to fences you pre-cut. Often, it's better to assemble the basic fence frame on the ground and raise it into place. This is easier to do if you work in sections.

Good cuts can be made in the field after the posts are set, by using a power saber saw or a bayonet saw. Sometimes, an insertion hole for the blade is required. A through mortise

can also be accomplished by boring two terminal holes and then cleaning out the waste stock with a keyhole or compass saw.

The advantage of field cuts is that frame-member positions can be accurately marked in relation to slope and other site conditions.

4. A few variations of the basic frame include:

• Locating post tops and top stringer 6" to 12" below the top of the sheathing. This reduces vertical span and the possible bowing of the sheathing.

• Extending the posts 6" to 12" above the top of the fence, for effect, does the same thing but creates an open panel by running a cap at the top of the posts.

• Installing a middle stringer for added strength. Actually it looks better if placed at the ⅔ mark than at the exact middle.

• Adding a 2" x 4" or 2" x 6" horizontal cap at the top of the fence. When this is done, the top stringer can be laid on edge and set in a notch cut in post tops.

• Using 4" x 6" or 6" x 6" posts and 4" x 4" or 2" x 6" stringers for a heavier scale and a sturdier frame.

5. Now is the time to stain the frame if a contrast between frame and sheathing is desired. It's a good idea to do any coloring job on the sheathing before it's nailed in place. The application of sheathing is usually a matter of holding in place and nailing. (See page 94 for nailing hints.)

Sheathing is usually installed in a vertical rather than a horizontal position because it makes better use of post spacing, spans from top to bottom with no splicing, and doesn't call as much attention to sloping ground.

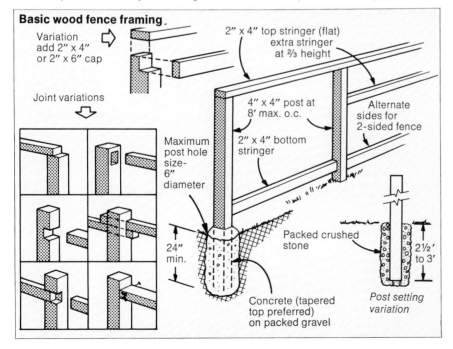

Basic wood fence framing.

Variation add 2" x 4" or 2" x 6" cap

2" x 4" top stringer (flat) extra stringer at ⅔ height

Joint variations

4" x 4" post at 8' max. o.c.

Alternate sides for 2-sided fence

Maximum post hole size— 6" diameter

2" x 4" bottom stringer

24" min.

Packed crushed stone

Concrete (tapered top preferred) on packed gravel

Post setting variation

2½' to 3'

A guide to fence and wall construction

Cost range is for six foot height, minimum 100 lineal feet, normal soil and access, all labor and materials by a contractor. Figure roughly one-half for materials only. Paint and stain extra. Rule-of-thumb for gates is five to ten times lineal foot cost. Distance from material source and manufacturer affects price considerably.

Type	Descriptions and Comments	Cost Range per lineal foot
Wood Fences	Typical frame: 4" x 4" posts set in concrete, maximum 8' on center, with 2" x 4" top and bottom stringers. Allow 50¢ per lineal foot for extra 2" x 4" stringer or cap.	
Grapestakes	Textural, weathers well, blends with shingle or shake roofs. Add cap for more sophisticated effect.	$4.00 to $6.00
Combed Stakes, 1" x 1"s, 1" x 2"s	More finished appearance than grapestakes. May need additional center stringer to prevent warping.	$4.00 to $7.00
Woven Palings	Smooth poles wired together. Natural appearing and quite sturdy.	$7.50 to $9.50
Boards	3" to 12" wide, ⅝" to 1"+ thick. Can be used in many different patterns and combinations. Roughsawn preferred in most gardens. Staining usually desirable.	$4.00 to $8.00
Louvers	Boards angled to exclude view, but allowing light and air to pass. Must be sturdily constructed.	$8.00 to $10.00
Woven Boards	Flexible boards installed in a basket-weaving manner. Often available pre-cut.	$4.00 to $6.00
Plywood	Patterned exterior siding types are best for outdoor use. Large panels are quickly nailed in place.	$4.00 to $8.00
Lath	4' standard length, and thinness (⅜") requires an extra stringer. Right angle or diagonal pattern.	$4.00 to $8.00
Picket	Should be related to house. Requires painting.	$3.00 to $4.00 (3' height)
Rail	Good for rustic settings and where solid barrier not needed.	$2.00 to $3.00 (3' height)
Shingles	Good way to cover up a structurally sound, but unattractive wood fence.	$5.00 to $6.00 (on existing frame)
"Custom"	Materials may not cost much more than for a basic fence, but labor can be prohibitive, unless built by the owner.	$10.00 and up
Chain-Link Fences	Typical frame: 1½" steel tubing posts set in concrete, maximum 10' on center. Heavy gauge wire top and bottom, or pipe top rail. Gates are sturdy, but unattractive.	
Standard Mesh	Best for background or covered by planting.	$4.00 to $5.00*
Colored Mesh	Less obtrusive than standard type. Black vinyl coating blends well with background.	$5.00 to $6.00*
Wood Inserts	Gives some degree of privacy and kills metal appearance.	$6.00 to $8.00
Plastic and Metal Inserts	Gives similar privacy as wood inserts, but can be garish.	$6.00 to $7.00
Wrought-Iron Fences	Typical Construction: Hollow steel tubing now used more than solid wrought-iron. 1" square posts are usually set 4' to 6' on center in concrete or bolted to paving. Uprights are normally ½" square tubing.	
Plain	Allows for view and air circulation. Excellent for swimming pool safety fence with uprights 4" apart.	$7.00 to $10.00
Patterned	Can be outstanding feature when related to house, but if overdone, detracts from serenity of garden.	$10.00 and up
Pre-Fabricated	Eliminates need for welding. Can be owner-installed.	$4.00 and up (3' height)

Type	Descriptions and Comments	Cost Range per lineal foot
Masonry Walls	Typical construction: Minimum 12" x 12" concrete footing, reinforcing steel @ 24" on center vertical, and horizontal in footing and top course. Grout solid all cells containing steel.	
Plain Concrete Block	Various sizes and thicknesses. 4" thick with pilasters, otherwise 6". Running bond is stronger than stacked. Needs planting to soften.	$6.00 to $8.00*
Colored Concrete Block	Usually more pleasing than plain gray. Buy all at one time to avoid color variations.	$6.50 to $8.50*
Special Concrete Block	Slump type, rough face, textural markings available. Some are quite handsome.	$7.00 to $9.00 *
Grille Concrete Block	Allows for design interest and view and air circulation. Can look "commercial."	$8.00 to $10.00*
Plaster over Concrete Block	Especially effective if ties in with architecture of house.	$7.00 to $9.00
Brick	Can be double wall, structural hollow brick or veneer over concrete block. Cost is main disadvantage. Many types and construction variations. Low walls more practical.	$10.00 to $15.00*
Stone	Many types and construction variations. Low walls more practical.	$5.00 to $10.00* (3' height)
Adobe	Obvious choice for adobe block house or patio.	$4.00 to $6.00* (3' height)
Poured Concrete	Forms must be very strong for 6' wall. Best use is for low seat walls.	$4.00 to $5.00 (seat wall)
Miscellaneous Fences	Typical wood framing can be used for most materials, with the addition of batting and bracing when needed.	
Glass	Allows view while blocking wind. Should be tempered plate glass for safety.	$10.00 and up*
Plexiglass	Same assets as glass and safer. Susceptible to scratching.	$10.00 and up*
Plastic	Standard fiberglass tends to look "cheap," doesn't wear well. Exterior grades of interior panels are sometimes available and more suitable for garden use.	$8.00 and up*
Bamboo	Individual canes require considerable labor to install. Rolls bound with sturdy wire preferred.	$8.00 to $10.00
Woven Reed	Good temporary screening. Can be added to chain-link, at very low cost.	$2.00 to $3.00 (on existing frame)
Wire-Mesh	Many different square and rectangular sizes and gauges. Main drawback is that it doesn't "spring" back when stretched out of shape.	$4.00 to $6.00
Expanded Metal	Sophisticated, but can look commercial. Natural or anodized aluminum better than painting.	$10.00 and up
Canvas	At home next to a swimming pool or at the beach. Vinyl coating extends life considerably.	$8.00 to $10.00
Stockade	Poles or timbers, usually buried part way in the ground with no other framework. Dramatic in the proper setting.	$10.00 and up
Plaster	Plaster on frame construction has been largely replaced by plaster over concrete block, since it appears the same and usually costs less.	$10.00 and up
Special Panels	Pebble textures, patterns and smooth surfaces can be seen at building supply and lumber yards. One-sided effect and high cost limits use.	$10.00 and up
Retaining Walls	Retaining walls can fail—with disastrous results. They should be properly engineered, or "overbuilt" for insurance. Low wood walls of decay resistant or pressure treated wood will last for a long time, but masonry construction is preferred.	$10.00 and up* (3' height)

* Because deeper footings are required in cold-winter regions, costs can be considerably higher.

Casual effect of grapestakes is ideal for natural gardens, requires little maintenance.

Fence of 1"x2"s drops down in height to allow view of hills.

Texture of pecky cypress adds interest to simple board fence.

1"x1"s give a neat appearance, help filter wind.

Grapestakes are a logical choice if you're looking for an economical sheathing that needs no special attention. The rough texture goes well with a ranch-like setting, but will appear more sophisticated if you place them points down and add a cap. Stakes with resawn vertical edges may be butted loosely against each other for maximum privacy.

Combed Grapestakes, 1" x 1"s and 1" x 2"s. These are a good alternative if grapestakes are just too rustic. Add a middle stringer for spans more than 3 feet to overcome bowing. A rough or resawn texture is preferred over surfaced lumber. Staining will enhance appearance. 2"x2"s are stronger, but cost more and have a "square" look that isn't always suitable. All can be spaced ½" apart for wind dispersal and air circulation if total privacy is not a factor.

Boards. Boards used for fencing range from ⅝" to 1" thick and 3" to 12" wide. House siding patterns such as tongue-and-groove and shiplap are sometimes used but need substantial framing and should be stained or painted to avoid unsightly cracks. Once again, a rough or resawn surface is usually preferred to finished lumber; the more finished in appearance a sheathing material is, the more evident cracks and other flaws will be.

Type, quality and cost vary greatly. Dry lumber is desirable since it will shrink less, but kiln-dried can be prohibitive in cost. Decay-resistant species and pressure-treated lumber seems to be less apt to warp and crack. Most fence companies and lumber yards handling fencing materials have displays of what type of boards are locally available. Look at both new and old constructions to see what kind of weathering effect you can expect.

Boards can be used in a great many patterns and combinations. Simplicity is usually best; busy, fancy patterns call attention to themselves.

Louvers. Boards placed at an angle afford privacy but still allow air to circulate and some light to pass through. Adjustable ones—made something like venetian blinds—can provide some degree of climate control. Judge advantages in relation to cost and effort to build. Most such jobs call for extra support, choice lumber and sturdy frames.

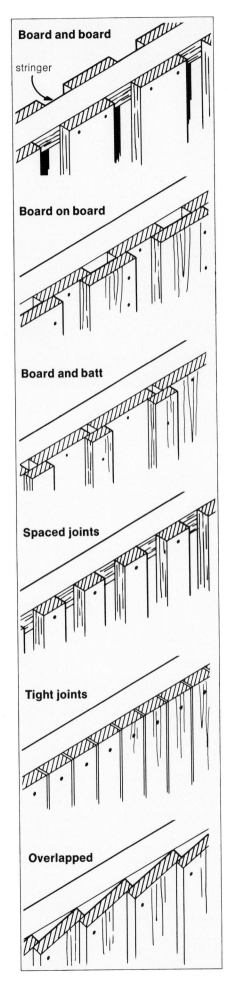

Board and board

stringer

Board on board

Board and batt

Spaced joints

Tight joints

Overlapped

Board-and-board fence allows air circulation, looks the same from either side.

Solid board-on-board fence offers total privacy. Gray stain suggests natural weathering.

Batts cover cracks and relieve flat surface in this board-and-batt fence.

Rough 2"x8" stringers give this low fence strength and distinction.

Stained tongue-and-groove resawn boards with black cap make a sophisticated, yet low maintenance fence.

Woven palings provide backdrop for an exotic garden scene.

Louvers allow light and air to pass through, but must be faced in right direction for privacy.

Shingles are a warm material and look good when used in a garden.

Woven board detail

Fence Board

1″ x 2″ or 2″ x 2″ Spacers

There are several ways to construct vertical louver fences:

Use 1″ x 4″ spacers nailed to the regular 2″ x 4″ stringers.

Notch oversize stringers in a saw-tooth pattern.

Horizontal louvers are installed similarly by nailing saw-tooth 1″ x 4″ spacers to the inside of the posts.

Wired Palings. These are similar to grapestakes, but are made from smooth poles that are wired together for easy installation. Half-round types are less expensive and more common than full-round, but the flat back side doesn't look as well as the front. "Cleft" woven has 1″± spaces between poles. Cost is considerably higher than grapestakes, except in areas near to manufacturers.

Woven Boards. Bender boards

(½″ x 4″) or plyable 1″ x 4″s or 1″ x 6″s can be used in a method similar to basketweaving. The simplest version consists of 4″ x 4″ posts at 8′ maximum on center, with no other framing. The boards are woven over one or more 1″ x 2″ or 2″ x 2″ center spacers to form an undulating pattern that provides privacy, looks the same from both sides, and admits light and air.

Any staining or painting should be done prior to assembly. A disadvantage of the design is that the horizontal strips form an easy-to-climb ladder.

Lath. ⅜″ thick x 1½″ wide lath doesn't work like grapestake or a 1″x6″ board, but it can serve in good fashion as light-weight fence material, when given support every 2′ or less. The material acquires strength when interlaced in a 45°, 60°, or 90° pattern,

and can span up to its full length of 4′ if nailed securely together. It can be used in a solid or open design. Use a spacing of 4″ to 6″ if you wish plants to grow through. The rough texture weathers quite well. But you can stain or paint if you wish.

Wired lath, available in 4′ high, 50′ and 100′ rolls, is excellent for temporary fences. Can be supported on regular 4″x4″ posts or on 1″ galvanized pipes driven into the ground.

Plywood. The biggest advantage of plywood for fencing is that you can cover large areas with single pieces. It's best to design the fence in relation to panel sizes to eliminate waste-cuts as much as possible.

Exterior grade plywood now comes in several different surfaces that adapt well to garden use. A rough-

White framework contrasts with painted lath to highlight climbing roses.

Tight woven fence, with verticals 12" apart also has 2"x4" cap.

This wood fence is a framework of 2"x4"s highlighted by an Oriental tile.

Natural lath panel attached to roof overhang provides both shade and privacy.

sawn or textured finish with vertical grooves of some type looks better than a smooth, unbroken surface.

Unfortunately, exterior plywood paneling only comes with one good side. If both sides of the fence are of equal importance, you can use two sheets of ⅜" plywood back-to-back (at double the cost). If one side is seen less than the other, use one ⅝"-thick sheet on the outside of the frame and paint or stain the backside. Also, you can add 2"x2" vertical or horizontal strips 6" apart on the back side to enhance appearance and to provide excellent support for climbing plants.

Vertical joints on exterior siding plywood interlock and do not require a cover batten (strip of wood over seam). Do use a batten if fence design causes a gap between panel edges.

It's wise to protect all plywood edges with a water-repellent preservative. A cap will provide additional protection for the top edge. The surface of some types can be left to weather, but staining is desirable. (See page 93 for additional information on plywood.)

Shingles. Houses with shingle siding are a natural for shingle fences, especially if they are wall-like extensions of the house itself. Shingles can be applied to the basic frame by adding 1"x4" nailing strips horizontally 6" on center. This allows for a 6" exposure to the weather. Start at the bottom and work up, measuring the placement of the 1"x4"s so the top course is approximately 6". A 2"x6" cap will overhang enough to give a neat, finished top.

The backside won't look the same as the front, but surprisingly it doesn't look too bad and is acceptable if softened with plants. Facing both sides with shingles is nice, but increases the cost.

Existing board fences that are structurally sound are easy to convert to a shingle fence. Standard shingle nails will show through most boards (and the 1"x4" nailers mentioned above). They should be cut off with nippers. Do this for safety as well as appearance.

Shingles are sold by the *square,* a quantity which covers 100 square feet of roof area. A square will cover a little bit more area when the shingles are applied to a vertical fence surface because more of the shingle is exposed.

Picket. Nothing seems quite as appropriate for some houses as a low, white picket fence. It's ornamental and also serves to keep traffic

This handsome fence was made by cutting 1"x8" boards with a band saw and nailing them 1" apart. Prevailing wind filters through the cracks.

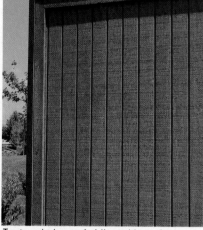

Textured plywood siding with vertical grooves makes strong fencing.

2"x2"s with spacers form an interesting screen.

Rough texture of 6' grapestake fence goes well with wall below. Using two materials helps reduce effective height.

Wind that used to swirl around the corner of the house is tamed by this grapestake wind screen.

off lawns and flower beds. Picket fences are seldom higher than 4'. To obtain some privacy simply add plants as a screen.

The basic frame, described earlier, applies to picket designs. Of course, it's lower, and the posts become part of the design. The posts are often cut to a special pattern similar to the pickets and extend about 6" above the top of the pickets. The top stringer is held down 6" or enough to clear the beginning of the picket head-shape.

If you have the power equipment (a band saw is fine), you'll probably enjoy shaping the pickets yourself, working with 1"x2", 1"x3", or 1"x4" standard widths. Pre-cut pickets are also available.

If traditional white paint is used, regular repainting will be necessary to keep a clean appearance. Use first quality paint to minimize the frequency. A paint roller works well on much of the surface.

Rail. Sometimes a fence is needed to define a boundary, without providing privacy or security. This is the place for a rail fence. Simplest form is a single rail, but two or three rails are more common.

Rustic types are done with split timber or poles for both the posts and rails. Posts are commonly set directly in the soil or packed with gravel. In "soft" soils they can sometimes be driven into the ground with a sledge hammer and a steel cap to protect the tops of the posts, or a special weighted post driver. Spacing is determined by size of the rails; it's normally 6' to 8'. Nailing a split timber or a pole to a post may call for drilling a pilot hole first. Double posts permit you to stack rails between them. A hole through the post lets you pass the rail through. This sort of mortise-and-tenon assembly is a frequently-used method.

Dimension lumber can also be connected with mortise-and-tenon joints for a modern post and rail fence. If you make the mortise double-height so rails overlap in the post, the joint will be stronger.

Rail fences can follow contours and still look fine. Also, they can zig-zag or meander without being visually disturbing.

Post-and-board fences use boards, usually 1"x6"s or 1"x8"s, as rails. These are frequently used for ranch and corral fences because they are inexpensive to install and single boards are easily replaced.

"Custom." There are almost limitless possibilities for "customizing" wood fences. You can apply moulding or special decorations, do cutouts, lattices, or shadow boxes, form egg-crate designs, use heavy timbers, telephone poles, or railroad ties—so much material can be used effectively if you plan the design well, and if the material is appropriate to the setting. Do consider though that a conversation-piece fence might outshine the rest of the garden.

Repairing a wood fence

You can reinforce an existing post when necessary, by digging a hole in front of the post and chipping away the concrete, to make room for a new one. Fill around the new post with concrete, and toenail or lag screw it to the old one. If you cut the new post short it will be less obvious.

A reinforcement post can be added between existing posts. Cut through the stringers to keep it from protruding, and to make it appear like part of the original project.

A 1½″ diameter steel pipe can also be used. Drive it with a sledge hammer next to the old post, just outside the concrete. Secure it to the post with plumber's tape and nails. You can add a wooden spacer between pipe and post if you wish. A 6′ length of pipe driven 2′ or 3′ into the ground is reasonably strong and won't show very much if painted to blend with the fence-color.

If the posts and frame are intact, shingles and other materials can be applied directly over existing sheathing—or—you can cover existing sheathing with new material.

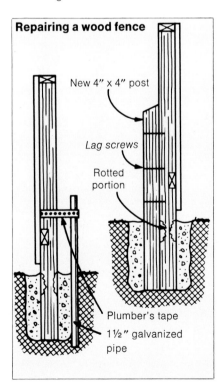

Repairing a wood fence

New 4″ x 4″ post

Lag screws

Rotted portion

Plumber's tape

1½″ galvanized pipe

White picket fence defines property and controls pets and children without giving a closed-in feeling.

Simple and sturdy, this fence is made by stacking 4″x4″s on top of a concrete foundation wall.

Split rail fences like this go all the way back to the 1700's. Mortise and tenon joint looks good and allows movement without breaking apart.

45

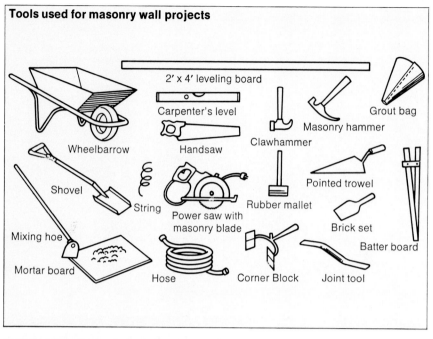

Tools used for masonry wall projects

2' x 4' leveling board

Carpenter's level

Wheelbarrow

Handsaw

Clawhammer

Masonry hammer

Grout bag

Shovel

String

Power saw with masonry blade

Rubber mallet

Pointed trowel

Brick set

Batter board

Mixing hoe

Mortar board

Hose

Corner Block

Joint tool

Concrete block wall construction

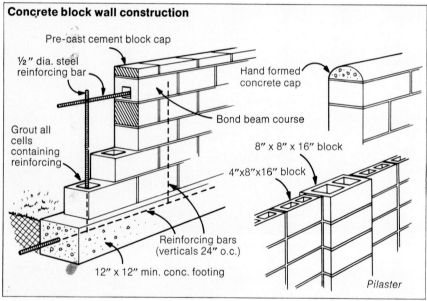

Pre-cast cement block cap

½" dia. steel reinforcing bar

Hand formed concrete cap

Bond beam course

8" x 8" x 16" block

4"x8"x16" block

Grout all cells containing reinforcing

Reinforcing bars (verticals 24" o.c.)

12" x 12" min. conc. footing

Pilaster

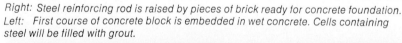

Right: Steel reinforcing rod is raised by pieces of brick ready for concrete foundation.
Left: First course of concrete block is embedded in wet concrete. Cells containing steel will be filled with grout.

Masonry walls

Masonry can be used very effectively in small or large gardens so long as the scale of the project is appropriate and the design is compatible. A 6' high, solid masonry perimeter wall on a small lot can give too much of a closed-in effect, while a lower wall topped with a wooden rail would not. Low concrete or brick walls surfaced with wood make good patio borders and provide extra seating. Such walls can be made hollow to serve as raised planters.

Masonry projects can be light or heavy in appearance, very formal or very rustic, solid or partially open. Many can be partly concealed with vines or shrubs. A brick wall with climbing vines has an attraction all its own.

Any homeowner with a desire to be a part-time mason will do well to visit a local builders supply yard to see the many modern materials that are available. Often, such places have mock-up walls and similar structures so you can get a good preview of an end result. This is a good way to check what you may have in mind, or simply to get ideas.

Typical Masonry Construction. Good footings and reinforcing are essential. General practice for a 6' high wall under normal conditions is a minimum 12"x12" concrete footing with ½" reinforcing steel rod at 24" on center vertical and one rod run horizontally in the footing and another in the bond beam course at the top of the wall. All cells or spaces containing steel are filled solidly with concrete grout.

For gates, set hinge bolts (and bolts on the opposite side of the opening to hold a latch board) in the mortar joints as the wall is being built.

Do bear in mind the importance of

and the help you can get from local building codes. Most building departments have professionally engineered specifications that take into consideration local conditions and requirements. These specs should be checked out and used on all projects.

Various soils pose special problems. Frost lines must be considered. Walls higher than 6' call for specific engineering. Walls that retain soil must be built strong enough to withstand heavy loads. They also need weep holes to relieve the build-up of hydrostatic pressure. It makes much sense to have a qualified person do the structural designing for you whenever you are in doubt about a project. You can still provide the labor.

Concrete Block. Concrete blocks are generally the most economical type of masonry wall. The units can be handled by one person (lightweight blocks such as cinder blocks weigh about 25 pounds, or half as much as a heavyweight type), yet are large enough to cover almost one square foot each. 8"x8"x16" or 6"x8"x16" are most commonly used, but 4" wide blocks can also be used by increasing the reinforcing and installing supporting pilasters 16' apart. (These 4" blocks are also usable as curbings, and planter walls up to 12" high.) The cells are convenient for reinforcing and grouting; there are shapes and sizes to meet almost any construction requirement; and there are innumerable options in regards to appearance.

Start by laying the wall out carefully. Have all the materials and tools on hand, and measure the distances involved to see how they fit the module of the blocks. (Physically laying out the blocks is the surest way).

Dig the foundation, taking care

that it doesn't extend beyond the property line. If the land is sloping, you may have to step the foundation in increments the same height as the block. Set the steel, soak the subsoil, pour the foundation and screed off for a level surface.

Pour the footing and allow it to cure first, then imbed the base course firmly in a 1" layer of mortar. Take plenty of time to get the first course straight and level. Space the blocks ½"± apart and fill the joints with mortar or leave partially open for weep holes if required. (See *Garden Floors and Decks* for concrete and mortar mixes.) A standard grout mix is 1 part cement, 2 parts sand, and 2 parts aggregate.

Lay the subsequent courses, buttering the edges of the blocks with mortar, setting in place and leveling by tapping gently with the handle of the trowel. Some practice beforehand is a good idea.

Build up corners first and then fill in between by working to string-line set up to guide the next course. Special metal line holders called "corner blocks" are helpful but you can simply tie the lines in place. For long runs, prop up the line in the middle to take care of sag. Use a long mason's or carpenter's level to plumb the corners.

Walls more than 50' in length should have an expansion joint to allow for expansion and contraction, or cracks are likely to occur.

Don't forget the steel reinforcing in the bond beam course. Special blocks with cut-outs for the bars are better than just laying them in the mortar. The top of the wall can be finished in several ways: With a solid cap block; a matching concrete brick or a clay brick cap; a flush or rounded concrete cap (fill all top cells with grout first by laying tar paper on the next to last

course to support it): or a 2" thick wood cap wide enough to overhang the wall slightly, and secured with bolts set in the grouted cells. The last is useful for low walls that might be used for sitting.

Strike the mortar joints before they get too hard to take a thumb print, by smoothing with a special joint-tool, or by using a short length of ¾" pipe, or by working with the trowel. Common joints are flush, weeping, rodded, or raked (deep cut) to emphasize the pattern. It's best to wait for mortar droppings to dry before you scrape them off with a trowel. If you try to clean up while the mortar is wet you will smear the material into the face of the block and it will become more difficult to remove.

Using or including colored, textured and patterned blocks can add much interest to many projects. The wall may be plastered to coordinate with a house finish or it can be painted with a cement base paint that both colors and adds a subtle texture.

Solid walls can be relieved by arranging some of the blocks with the cells sideways or by spanning over an open space. There are also many grille blocks available. Allowance must be made in either case for additional reinforcing to compensate for loss of strength because of the openings.

Random placement of any kind of different block can look spotty and often detracts more than it adds. Carrying through with all one type, or introducing contrasting sections is generally more effective.

Concrete block walls can also be combined with other materials. To reduce the apparent height of a 6' wall, the lower 4' can be block, with 2' of wood on top. Wrought-iron grilles can be used as panels to permit a glimpse through an otherwise solid barrier.

Split-face type concrete block gives stone-like appearance at much less expense.

Half blocks turned sideways form a grille panel in this colored concrete block wall.

Timbers bolted to slump type concrete block add a bold accent.

Pierced brick wall of "rug-face" bricks is more interesting than a solid wall.

Oversized bricks 12" long x 4" high are well scaled for long, low wall.

Brick wall construction

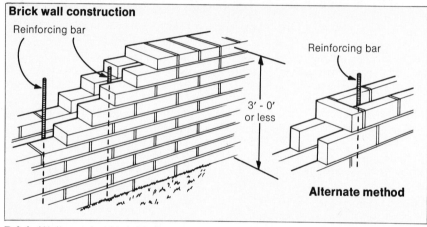

Reinforcing bar

Reinforcing bar

3' - 0' or less

Alternate method

Adobe block wall has pilaster for additional strength.

Brick. Walls made of brick take more time to do than those of concrete block simply because bricks are smaller, and most don't have open cells in which to place reinforcing steel and grout. This means that a double wall is normally used which adds up to 16 bricks instead of one concrete block. (Hollow structural bricks and brick tiles are available in some areas, but solid bricks prevail.)

In addition to more time, having to use a double wall raises the cost of the bricks to approximately double that of block. For many, the warmth and beauty of brick is more important than money, and as with garden paving, brick walls continue to be a favorite. A good compromise is to limit brick walls to planter boxes, seats and low walls, unless you can find hollow structural bricks.

Essentially, brick walls are constructed the same as concrete block. Actually it's easier to apply the mortar because it's furrowed-out on top of the course below with a pointed trowel so that only one end of the brick needs to be "buttered." The bricks must be wet down before use for a good bond; adding concrete glue to mortar for caps that might be knocked loose will provide extra strength. The choices as to type of trowel joints are the same — plus a lot more of them.

One common construction method is to build two parallel walls one brick wide, laid flat, leaving a ½"± crack between for reinforcing steel and thin mortar grout. This allows an 8" wide cap course of bricks laid flat or on edge.

Laying all the bricks on edge takes fewer bricks and leaves 3½"± inside for steel and grouting. However, it isn't as strong unless some of the bricks are placed cross-wise as a header course. Lay out a dry sample first, since the effect is quite different. Pilasters approximately 12' apart are commonly provided for brick walls more than 3' high.

A single row of bricks can be used for curbings and planters up to 12" high if pargeted (applying a face coat of mortar to the back side) for added strength.

If only one side is exposed, a poured concrete or a concrete block wall can be veneered with bricks. Corrugated metal masonry ties should be installed in the wall to be covered. When applying brick veneer over an existing wall, these ties can be secured to the wall with concrete nails.

Low walls that retain soil should be built more strongly by enlarging the footing and adding reinforcing. All retaining walls more than 30" high should be professionally engineered.

Adobe. "Slump" type concrete blocks have replaced adobe as a wall building material in all but a few areas in the southwest. The concrete counter-part looks similar, is stronger, is readily available, and is easier to lay.

Still, for those living in a rustic ranch house, especially if constructed of adobe blocks, the authentic material is likely to be preferred.

Aside from being bigger and heavier, adobe blocks are laid very

Brick (above) and stone (below) are veneered over concrete block backing.

Stone wall in ashlar pattern shows excellent craftsmanship.

Rubble stone wall with recessed joints to highlight individual stones.

much like brick walls. They are, however, not as strong, and footings, reinforcing and mortar should allow for this fact. To be on the safe side, it's a good idea to procure a plan to work from: some excellent publications are available from agricultural extension services in states where adobe is used. See page 96.

Stone. Laying concrete blocks and bricks is a craft; creating stone walls is an art.

Having a source of inexpensive stone is a good excuse to do a stone wall. You may live near a quarry, or even have usable stone on your property. Rounded and irregular stones *can* be used for wall construction, but stratified types that can be laid in courses and are more easily trimmed are better. Most important, the stone should be stable enough to withstand the type of weather it will be subjected to.

Lightweight, volcanic stone that can be sawed or chiseled, is a good choice for natural effect. With careful fitting, joints can be made almost invisible;

an extremely difficult task with hard stone.

Stone can be laid in two basic ways: in courses *(ashlar)*, or not in courses *(rubble)*. The flatter and more regular the stone, the more it is like laying block or brick. The more rounded or irregular, the more mortar that is required and will show.

Stone slabs can be laid vertically as a veneer over poured concrete or concrete block walls. This is an efficient use of the material because the "thin" coating of stone covers a maximum area. However, unless carefully done, the wall can have a "glued-on" appearance, and lose the character associated with solid stone.

Some special characteristics of stone wall construction are that stone walls are almost always built with a batter (an inward slope of ½ to 1″ per foot of vertical height); more large stones are used in the lower portion for stability and appearance; and

strength is dependent upon headers (stones set at right angles to the face of the wall), overlapping, and careful mortaring. Other than that, the basic principles of typical masonry construction should be followed, except that stone walls more than 3′ high should be reserved for experts.

In addition to conventional walls, stone can also be laid dry. They must be positioned carefully, so as to hold each other in place by sheer weight alone. Batter should be a minimum of 1″ per foot of vertical height. This method can also be used to build a low retaining wall (usually 3′ or less) with plants growing in the crevices for a casual effect. Tilting the stones slightly back into the soil helps hold moisture and is stronger.

Broken concrete is an inexpensive material that adapts well to dry-wall construction and gives a stone-like effect. (See chapter on *Recycled and Inexpensive Materials.*)

Waterfall tumbles over stone wall laid directly on top of swimming pool wall. Landscape Architect, L. Ken Smith.

Low, poured concrete wall protects narrow planting bed from paved area traffic.

Wood inserts give more privacy to a chain-link fence.

Planter box of poured concrete highlights corner of swimming pool and shields plants from chlorine water.

Black vinyl coating helps chain-link fence blend with background.

Poured concrete. The big job here is building the forms. This almost always takes more time than the actual pour, but results can be worth it especially when concrete is used in a manner that emphasizes its fluidity in sweeping curves and free forms.

High walls, especially retaining walls should not be designed by an amateur. Seat walls, curbings, and small retaining walls are okay but even here design should be checked against local codes.

Poured concrete is strong, and 6″ to 8″ is thick enough for most garden walls. However, wider walls (up to 18″ for seat types) invariably look better and seem to be well suited to the nature of the material.

Prepare the footing much the same as for a block wall. Then begin the forming. Plywood (½″ or thicker) is a good material, especially if a smooth surface is desired. For curves, ¼″ plywood or hardboard bends fairly well; sheet metal is good for a tight radius. 1″ thick lumber can be used for both straight runs and gentle curves if sufficiently staked as all forms should be.

Common stakes are 1″x3″, and 2″x4″s, nailed vertically against the form boards & secured with diagonal braces driven into the soil and securely staked. The forms must be strong enough to hold the concrete, and some consideration must be given to easy removal. Don't let nails protrude on the inside of forms; use double headed nails for easy pulling. A light coat of clean oil or an application of commercial form ''release'' will eliminate adhesion between concrete and wood.

Reinforcing steel should be suspended with tie wires running through cracks or holes drilled in the forms so that it remains in position during pouring. The wires are almost undetectable when cut off flush.

Be sure the subsoil is well soaked, then pour in one continuous (monolithic) mass, moving in 6″ layers from one end of the forms to the other. Ready-mix concrete may be a good way to go for all but the smallest jobs. Tamp the concrete as it is poured but not so much that you push all large aggregate to the bottom. Screed off the top and tap the forms with a hammer to force the large aggregate back from the outside surfaces. Finish the top with a wood trowel and an edger when it has set up sufficiently to work.

Forms can be carefully stripped from curbings and low walls while the concrete is still green, and the surface finished with a brush and a mixture of sand and cement. However, once the forms are removed, the concrete is vulnerable to damage, or worst yet, if they are removed too soon, the wall may end up looking like a fallen cake. It's safer to leave the forms on for several days, wetting occasionally with a hose, and touching-up any imperfections later.

Chain-Link
Chain-link fencing offers maximum visibility, adapts with little difficulty to

Simple wrought-iron fence is installed in sections between masonry piers.

Wrought-iron fence painted black gives protection for swimming pool area without cutting out view.

irregular land, keeps out intruders and all but the smallest animals, is extremely long-lived, allows air and light to pass through, and is an excellent support for plants.

It does not, however, offer privacy in itself. It does allow sound to pass through, as well as water and weed seeds, and its "industrial" appearance is often objectionable.

Variations might overcome some of the objections. Wood inserts, if you can make or find some to fit, give a degree of privacy and look surprisingly good. Plastic and metal inserts do add privacy, but contribute a highway look.

Vinyl covered fabric in dark green and black will help the fence blend into the background. Posts and rails should be painted to match the color of the vinyl.

The galvanized steel tubing posts are set in concrete like wood posts, but may be spaced 10′ on center and a minimum of 2½′ deep. Corner posts are subjected to a considerable pull and should be 2″ outside diameter; line posts can be 1⅝″ o.d. Allow posts to set up for a week before attaching fabric.

A top rail 1⅜″ o.d., slipped through a special loop cap, adds strength. Instead of a second rail, a heavy gauge wire is run 2″± from the bottom. It's possible to substitute a second wire for the top rail.

Fabric should be 2″ galvanized wire mesh, minimum 11 gauge, or 9 gauge for extra strength. It's attached at one end to tension bars held in place

with bolted tension bands. Then a special fence stretcher (rentable, and often loaned by the people who sell the fence material) is used to pull the fabric while you connect to another tension bar at the other end.

Contractors in this area are quite efficient and are competitive. It might pay to get some bids before you tackle the project.

Wrought-Iron

Wrought-iron is a good choice for a see-through fence when safety and security are desired along with beauty. Typical applications are for pool safety—fencing, gates, view panels set in a solid fence, and railings. Initial cost and need for painting are main drawbacks.

Custom-made wrought-iron can be ordered with installation by the owner in mind. This, of course, calls for very careful measuring. Prefabricated modules are designed for easy installation with bolted connectors. Choice, however, is pretty much limited to low fencing and railings.

Posts are usually 1″ tubular steel and can be set 24″ deep in concrete (4″ diameter holes are ample), or in 2″ diameter holes drilled in existing masonry and filled with quick-set cement. Floor flanges can also be used on wood or masonry, but allowance for vertical rigidity may be needed.

Fancy patterns are tempting, but simple uprights do the job just as well, and may look better at lower cost.

Brick wall and wrought-iron is a pleasing combination; doesn't appear as heavy as a solid wall.

Miscellaneous Fences

If you're considering some unique type of fencing, keep in mind that there may be a valid reason why it is uncommon. High cost and inability to withstand outdoor conditions eliminate many promising candidates. The basic wood frame can be modified to accommodate the following:

Glass—should be ¼" tempered plate for safety. Blocks the wind without cutting-off the view. Install with perimeter moulding strips and allow ample space for movement.

Plexiglass—has the same advantages as glass and is less susceptible to shattering. Shows scratch marks.

Plastic—lets the light through, while blocking the wind and giving privacy. Fiberglass tends to age and some-times looks "cheap" and foreign in a garden setting. Some exterior grade panels are quite handsome.

Bamboo—is easier to install in wire-bound rolls, rather than individual pieces. Lasts a long time if clear of the ground, but discolors and cracks with age.

Woven reed—is a cheap version of bamboo and deteriorates in a year or so. Often applied to a chain-link fence for summer privacy.

Canvas—will last for five or more years if vinyl coated. This is another good summer privacy addition for chain-link.

Asbestos-cement—comes in both flat and corrugated panels. Natural gray is all right with some color schemes, and can be stained or painted if desired. Thin panels are easily shattered, but ¼" thick ones, especially if corrugated, are quite strong.

Welded-wire mesh—is a good way to combine wood posts and see-through fencing. Comes all the way from ½" to 6" squares, plus rectangular shapes, and in various gauges. Easy to install with heavy ¾" staples; 1"x2" or wider wood batts can be added to cover the sharp edges. Doesn't spring back once it's been pushed out of shape.

Expanded metal—can be used for a sophisticated effect, with see-through quality dependent upon specific pattern. Should be galvanized or aluminum or painted.

Special panels—pressed wood chips, fibers in a cement base, pebbles

Translucent white plastic and black wood fence gives privacy without blocking light, and coordinates with other materials.

Cement and fiber panels on steel pipes form a contemporary backdrop for sculpture and pottery.

Corrugated asbestos-cement panels will not warp or deteriorate. Steel pipes will last longer than wood posts.

Canvas panels within 2"x10" wood frame add rich color and deflect wind. Landscape architect: Roy H. Seifert.

applied with epoxy over plywood, and other products are sometimes usable for fencing. The ones that hold up well outdoors are usually considerably more expensive than standard paneling.

There are several additional types of fencing that don't use the basic frame.

Plaster over wood frame—that is constructed like a house, was once a common garden wall in parts of the west. It's still occasionally used, but plaster over concrete block, or slump type block is now prevalent.

Stockade—type walls built of logs, telephone poles or railroad ties sunken part way in the ground in the manner of an old-time fort, are a striking way of enclosing an area. For a 6′ fence, dig a 3′ deep trench,

set the pieces vertically, pack the earth firmly to hold in place, and toenail together for added strength. The tops can be level, or irregular for a more primitive appearance. Low walls are effective and can be used for retaining soil. (See *Recycled and Inexpensive Materials*.)

Columns—of concrete block, brick, stone, or heavy timbers as described above, can be used instead of conventional posts, with paneling in between. They should relate to overall design and scale, or they can look overpowering.

Adding-on to a fence—
You can increase the height of a fence by adding a lightweight material to its top. (Property owners that back up to a busy street or highway should make sure there are no restrictions

before building their fence higher. Be considerate too, and check with neighbors.)

A 2′ tall addition of plastic, lath or stakes is easy to add, and is in proportion to a 6′ fence. 2″x4″ framing can be nailed directly on top of most wood fences. Just make a box with a 2″x4″ upright every 6′ to 8′. Attach a 2″x4″ or 2″x6″ sill to the top of a masonry wall by drilling for and setting expansion shields for bolts. Then proceed as if it were a wood fence. Extending a 2″x4″ down the face of the fence and protruding 2′ above gives a more rigid support if firmly bolted to the fence or wall.

Solid panels can act as a sail, and should only be added to fences strong enough to withstand the additional wind load.

Textured plastic sheets screen a bathroom garden from view.

Wood fence on top of existing concrete block wall increases privacy.

2″x2″s bolt to existing concrete block wall to support wood fence added to top.

Lath added to top of existing wood fence gives privacy from nearby 2-story houses. Wind passes through lath and doesn't add a strain to the solid fence.

Plastic added to top of a concrete block wall blocks out view from street without appearing oppressive.

Two 2"x4"s extend and bolt to roof rafters to serve as a strong gate post.

Back of same gate showing 2"x4" "Z" brace, heavy "T" hinges and string pull latch.

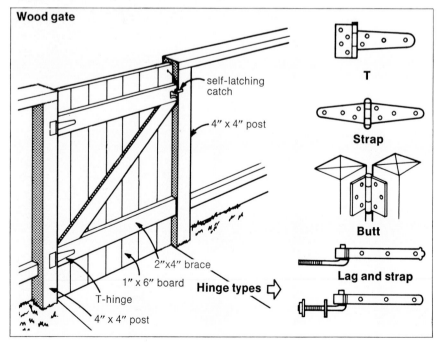

Low gate is split into two sections with a cane bolt in center.

Wood gate

self-latching catch

4" x 4" post

2"x4" brace

1" x 6" board

T-hinge

4" x 4" post

Hinge types ⇨

T

Strap

Butt

Lag and strap

Gates

A well-designed and properly installed gate will not bind or sag or break down. There are many situations that call for a gate but this should not lead you into installing one at every opening. Often, an off-set baffle can screen a service area, for example, and eliminate the need for a section of fence you must constantly open and close. A gate across the driveway might sound nice but do consider its cost and the nuisance of having to leave the car to get to it.

"Make the gates wide enough and strong enough and a customer will overlook practically anything else," said an experienced fencing contractor. A gate is a practical project and design considerations should relate to that fact. You can squeeze through 2' but suppose you need to wheel through a wheelbarrow or lawn mower, or the like? 3' might do as a minimum but something between that and 6' is better. Often, you can do with a two-part gate; one section remains closed until you need extra passage width. Extra width—say about 4'—might be considered at a front entrance simply because it is more gracious.

Weight is the enemy of a successful gate. Some gates more than 4' feet wide get so heavy that sagging is difficult to avoid. The two-part gate we mentioned is one solution. Another out is to install a runner wheel for outboard support. This is almost a necessity for single-hung driveway gates that span 8' or more.

Make gates of the same material as the fence whenever possible. If privacy isn't a requirement, you can add open grillwork to an entrance gate to make it more inviting. Strictly utilitarian gates can be designed to blend in with the fencing to reduce visual impact.

Typical wood gate construction

1. Measure the opening. If it's out of plumb, see if it can be straightened. If not, make adjustments in the gate itself. Allow ½" for hinge clearance, and another ½" on the latch side. If the posts aren't sturdy enough to support a gate, strengthen them before proceeding.

2. Select straight, light, dry lumber. Lay out three 2"x4"s flat in a "Z" pattern (with the hinges to the left; reverse the "Z" if hinges are to the right). Nail the paneling on the outside, using more nails than for the fencing.

3. Place the gate in the opening, on blocks if necessary, and mark the hinge locations. Use heavy-duty hinges and secure them with maximum-length screws or use bolts. Hang the gate and test it for swing and fit.

4. Install the latch. Add a strip as a door stop to hide the crack, if the gate swings only one way.

The gate can also be built as a box using a frame of 2"x4"s on edge, and a diagonal 2"x4" brace. This is good design for lightweight sheathing that needs edge support. A heavy gauge wire with a turnbuckle can be substituted for the wood brace, or added for greater strength. It is run in the opposite direction as the 2"x4" diagonal. Steel angle braces may be added to strengthen joints.

You can turn an existing chain-link gate into a strong wood gate by applying sheathing to 1"x4" nailers bolted to the steel frame.

Wrought-iron gates are both strong and attractive. As with chain-link, wood can also be added if a solid barrier is desired.

Whenever possible, hang gates from house walls rather than free standing posts. Use three ½"x7" lag bolts into studs to attach a 4"x4" to a frame-house wall. (A 4"x4" offers more room to attach a hinge than a 2"x4".) Work with expansion shields for attachments to a masonry wall.

Add a door closer for pool enclosures, and where children or pets might slip out through a gate that is left ajar. The simplest type is a heavy spring especially designed for gate use. Install it on the inside so it will be unobtrusive.

When a padlock is too big a nuisance on a gate that must be locked, you can use a bolt-action latch or chain latch on the inside.

A dead-bolt keyed on the outside and with a thumb-latch or keyed lock on the inside has the advantage of being lockable from the outside when leaving the premises.

Rectangular pattern adds interest to this wood gate and relates it to fence panels.

Dead-bolt is easy to install in wood gate, allows convenient locking without padlock.

Above: Wrought iron gate spans driveway without sagging. Note that diagonal steel rod brace is under tension and runs downhill from hinge side. Below: Plastic attached to back of wrought iron gate maintains airiness while providing privacy.

Decorative wrought-iron fits archway; is appropriate selection for style of house.

Above: Shade structures don't have to be dark and oppressive. This one is light and airy. Landscape architect, Barbara Fealy. Below: This dramatic shade structure is effective in the fog as well as on sunny days.

Pergolas, arbors, shade structures and gazebos

There are several types of garden structures that can add to your outdoor living enjoyment.

They're known loosely under such names as pergolas, arbors, bowers, ramadas, lath houses, overheads, egg-crates, shade shelters and gazebos. Whatever you choose to call them, their primary purpose is to break the intensity of the sun for the comfort of the people below.

Some auxiliary benefits are to give a feeling of partial enclosure, add a structural element in scale with the garden, and to offer support for climbing vines and protection for shade-loving plants.

Shade structures

A shade structure can serve several purposes at one time, and can be modified as family needs change. It's a good sand-box and tricycle area for pre-schoolers by day, and a place for adults to sit and relax in the evening. Adding a table makes it usable for hobbies for young and old. A radio or record player can provide music. It can be a place for additional "indoor" gardening and it can become a type of greenhouse.

The characteristics that differentiate shade structures from solid roof construction is that they don't provide protection from rain, and they permit free air circulation. Paving of some type is a good idea for maximum usability.

Always check local building codes to see if a permit is required and to learn about restrictions. Clauses in some codes exempt a free-standing pergola not over 400 square feet in area from jurisdiction, as long as it complies with the required zoning setbacks. Of course, any structure should be built strongly enough to be safe. Use flammable coverings with caution; fire department regulations may govern material and spacing.

Protection for plants is the primary purpose of this construction.

Grapes are being trained on this sturdy arbor.

This outdoor living area would be unusable without the shade structure.

Attached shade structure

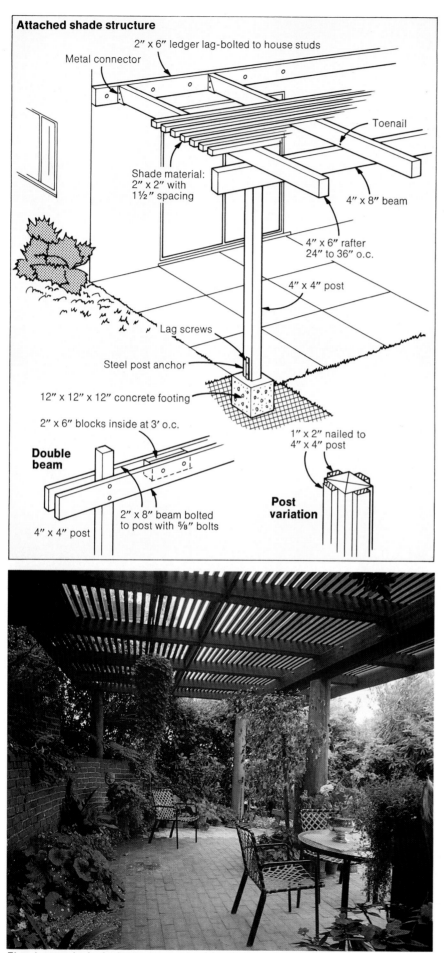

2" x 6" ledger lag-bolted to house studs

Metal connector

Toenail

Shade material: 2" x 2" with 1½" spacing

4" x 8" beam

4" x 6" rafter 24" to 36" o.c.

4" x 4" post

Lag screws

Steel post anchor

12" x 12" x 12" concrete footing

2" x 6" blocks inside at 3' o.c.

Double beam

4" x 4" post

2" x 8" beam bolted to post with ⅝" bolts

1" x 2" nailed to 4" x 4" post

Post variation

There's room for both plants and people under this long shade trellis.

Attached

Shade structures offer two distinct advantages: The house wall gives excellent support, eliminating half the posts; and it's more convenient to use.

It's recommended that attached structures be built at least strong enough to support the weight of a person. Anticipate the possible addition of solid roofing at some later date. (A pitch for water runoff will be appreciated by a future roofer.)

Construction is similar to that of a solid roof except the rafters are more prominent and look better if they are larger and spaced farther apart. Where a patio roof might use 2"x6" rafters spanning 10' at 16" on center, 4"x6"s at 24" to 36" apart are more appropriate for a shade structure. (Use 4"x8" rafters for spans up to 12'. Refer to building department charts or consult with an architect for longer spans or extraordinary conditions.)

Egg-crating involves cross-pieces between the rafters for extra strength and for appearance. They must be installed neatly to keep from appearing crooked. Egg-crating throws little shade but offers good support for materials laid on top.

Posts are normally 4"x4"s of decay resistant wood, spaced 8' apart for a 4"x8" beam, 10' for a 4"x10", etc. Double clasping beams are interesting and can be used if securely bolted together through 16" long, 2"x6" spacer blocks placed 3'± apart. The

Rafter end designs

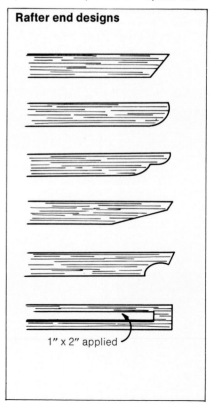

1" x 2" applied

posts are supported by a minimum 12" sq. footing extending 12" into undisturbed earth, and bolted in place with a steel post anchor or similar device. 6"x6"s and various combinations of built-up wood posts, or 2" (round or square) galvanized steel pipe columns are also used. (Wood beams are attached to steel posts with floor flanges threaded to a round pipe, or welded saddles.)

Sometimes the rafters can be connected directly to existing house rafters or the fascia. A stronger method (and required by most codes) is to lag bolt a 2"x6" ledger directly to the house wall with ½"x5½" lag bolts into every other stud. Attach to a masonry wall by bolting into expansion shields inserted in holes drilled with a masonry bit.

Unless built into an "L" or "U" of the house, some shear support is required to eliminate sway in a direction parallel to the house wall. 45° knee braces at each post will do the job, but are head bumpers and may look like an afterthought unless they are designed as decorative details like a brace cut from a 4"x6". Lag-bolted steel "T" braces are often used to tie posts and beams together, and offer shear support.

Steel or aluminum pipe framing is frequently used for canvas, and is also suitable for other rollable coverings such as saran shade cloth. The effect is special—entirely different than wood construction—but appropriate in certain situations.

Outdoor ping-pong is a pleasure on this shady patio. 2"x2"s are spaced 2" apart to allow air circulation.

Heavy steel "T" ties post and beam together and reduces side sway.

Wood deck and shade trellis create comfortable sitting area at edge of swimming pool.

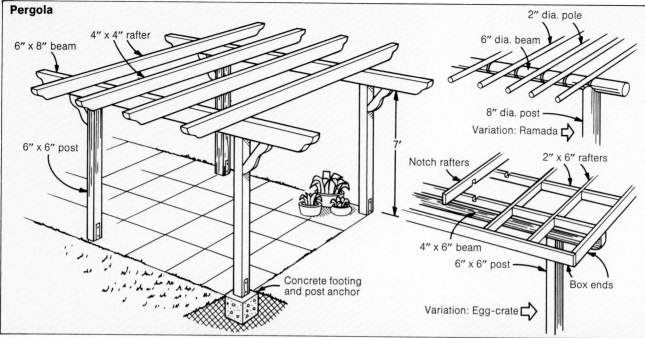

Pergola

6" x 8" beam

4" x 4" rafter

6" x 6" post

Concrete footing and post anchor

7'

2" dia. pole

6" dia. beam

8" dia. post

Variation: Ramada

Notch rafters

2" x 6" rafters

4" x 6" beam

6" x 6" post

Box ends

Variation: Egg-crate

Ramada of peeled logs is sophisticated version of old time cowboy shelters. Landscape architect, Jon F. Myhre.

Neat, simple design characterizes this poolside lath house for people.

Pergola of heavy timbers supports grapes and climbing roses.

Lath house has side walls in addition to covering on top.

Free-standing

Open garden structures of heavy scale are usually termed pergolas and are especially effective if compatible with the architecture of the house. Arbors and bowers are similar but are generally of lighter construction and often covered with vines.

Free-standing projects require a minimum of four posts in two rows. A rectangular form using six posts is preferred over a square if space is available.

Shear bracing in two directions is needed to keep free-standing structures such as pergolas and arbors from swaying.

The ramada. In the southwestern United States and Mexico, the "ramada" is used to block the relentless sun of arid desert regions. The classic design consists of irregular logs sunk in the ground as posts to support log beams. Poles, made from stripped branches are tied to the top with leather thongs or fiber rope. Ocotillo and cholla branches, palm leaves, reeds and yucca flower stalks are also used for the shade covering.

Such a structure may be a bit too picturesque for the average garden. However, you can use uniform logs and poles, and bolted post-and-beam construction, to make the ramada more compatible while still retaining the spirit and romance of the original.

The lath house differs from other shade structures in that it is more for plants than for people. It usually has some vertical walls to filter the wind. and to provide additional shade. Also, smaller dimensioned lumber, such as 2"x4"s and 4"x4s" can be used and still be in scale with the lath.

The gazebo. Remove some of the plants, add benches and people, and the lath house becomes a gazebo. It can be of classic Victorian design, painted white and complete with scroll work and turned posts; or it can be as contemporary as you desire.

Hexagonal or octagonal shapes are popular, but a square is easier to build. A gazebo need not be large; coziness is preferred over spaciousness. Lay out an 8' square or a 10' diameter circle and test it for size. Keeping it small makes it possible to retain a light, airy effect, since it eliminates the need for heavy timbers.

If you want to build an elaborate gazebo, it's best to start by buying a complete set of plans. Another option is to buy a pre-cut kit that you assemble. Look in garden magazines for companies supplying such materials.

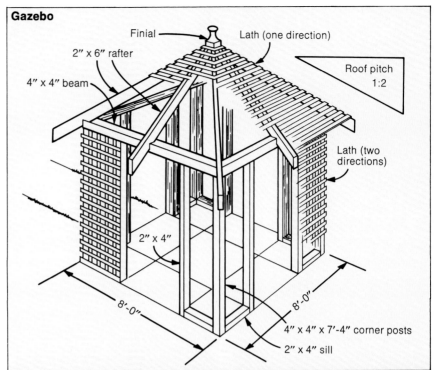

Gazebo

Finial — Lath (one direction)

2" x 6" rafter

4" x 4" beam

Roof pitch 1:2

Lath (two directions)

2" x 4"

8'-0"

8'-0"

4" x 4" x 7'-4" corner posts

2" x 4" sill

Custom-welded steel plate simplifies connection of six gazebo rafters.

Arbor is raised to take advantage of view. Note double 2" x 8" beams.

Poolside gazebo offers views in all directions. Wrought-iron panels are simple to add to wood framing.

Reflected heat from paving overheats house and offers no cool place to sit.

Carborundum blade is used to cut through existing asphalt paving for post footing.

Post is bolted to steel post anchor set into a concrete footing.

Attach post to existing concrete with a surface grip held by ½″ expansion bolt.

2″ x 6″ ledger is attached to house wall with 5½″ lag screws into studs.

Beam is toe-nailed to post which will be covered with 1″ x 6″ facing board.

2″x2″s are stained with a 7″ nylon spread painter before installing—much easier than doing when they're up in the air.

Completed shade trellis provides an interesting design to the house elevation as well as a comfortable shaded place for lounging or barbecuing under the extended area. Design—Kenneth Myers.

Building a shade structure

1. Lay out the footings carefully, remembering to measure to the center of the posts. If an inspection is required, get it well in advance of the pouring date. Have post anchors ready for insertion. After pouring, allow several days for the footings to cure unless using pre-cast piers. Concrete paving is normally poured the same time as the footings. Other types of paving can be laid before or after the shade structure is built.

2. For attached structures, secure the ledger to the wall, so it will be ready for the rafters.

3. Cut the posts to correct length and set in position, bracing in two directions with 2"x4"s, 6' or 8' long. Measure carefully before sawing off the posts, allowing for the depth of the beam if it is to be set on top of the posts, and roof pitch, if any. Raise the beam(s) and attach to the posts. Arrange for some help; trying to wrestle a heavy beam into place alone is dangerous. Have extra wood on hand to use as temporary braces.

4. Install the rafters but be sure to cut any decorative end design, while they are still on the ground. (Metal connectors make it easy to attach directly to the face of the ledger rather than setting the rafter on top.)

5. Check plumb and level and correct deviation. Then bolt or nail shear braces into position.

6. Attach shade material on top of the rafters. If staining or painting wood strips, do it on the ground before installing.

Coverings

The denseness of shade cast is determined by what material and what spacing is used on top of the rafters. The rafters themselves can be enough if a vine is to be trained over the top. For both summer shade and winter sun, the material should be easily removable.

Saran shade cloth comes in a range of shade density and can be held in place with grommets or wood batts. It's easy to remove and roll up for winter storage. Leave a slight billow to allow for shrinkage.

Woven reed and bamboo in rolls may be installed or removed quickly. They throw a pleasing mottled shade, and are reasonable in cost. Bamboo will last longer than reed and is especially strong when the binding is wire rather than string.

Window screen, louver screen, woven plastic webbing, and various types of netting can also be used over a basic framework for different shade densities.

Top: Plastic shade cloth comes in many densities and patterns; can be added to existing framework. Bottom: Woven reed is ideal for shade plants; is inexpensive enough to replace when it deteriorates.

Above left: These 2" x 2"s are spaced 4" apart. Adding another 2" x 2" in between would increase shade considerably. Above right: Rafters silhouetted against the sky are pleasing to look through. Below: 1" x 2"s laid flat with 1½" spaces between may throw a "zebra" pattern in areas with extremely bright sunshine.

Trellis of lath arches blocks afternoon sun and adds character to an otherwise uninteresting facade.

4"x6" rafters continue under house overhang and attach to 2"x6" ledger at the house wall.

Shear bracing to prevent sway is turned into design feature by use of four braces at each post.

Metal connectors can be used for almost any type of wood joint; are stronger than just nailing.

Sun grille is simple to add to an existing overhang. 2" x 3"s are notched and extend in front of plaster wall.

Steel post anchor embedded in concrete footing prevents moving and lifting of post.

Wood strips are more permanent, and more variable in the amount of shade they give. A good test for all kinds is to lay out an area after the frame is built to see how far apart they should be in order to give the desired amount. In areas of brilliant sunshine, an eye-dazzling zebra pattern may be created, making close spacing or the addition of another material on top of the wood necessary. Wood strips can be built in panels to change the position of the shade, and for removal when the sun is desired. Storage is more of a problem than with rollable materials.

Lath is the old standard shade giver. Limit the span to 24" unless they are woven or nailed together, in which case full 4' lengths can be used. Cost is nominal and the effect pleasing.

Grapestakes can be used like lath, and have the advantage of spanning up to 6' with little sag. They relate well to shake roofs and ranch style houses.

1"x1"s, 1"x2"s, 2"x2"s, 2"x3"s and so on, can be used for a more finished effect. The larger dimensions are more in scale with heavy framing. Cost increases greatly when going into 2" thick pieces.

The eyebrow

Another type of shade structure is a cantilevered eyebrow that extends the roof line to shade a window or a wall that receives too much sun. The idea is much the same as a canvas awning, except that by using wood, the addition can be made to look like it belongs with the house.

For western exposures, the eyebrow idea can be used in a vertical position as a window grille, in order to block late afternoon sun.

If the house rafter tails are exposed, they can often be extended with a bolted-on 2"x4". Clasping it with two 2"x4"s will make it more symmetrical. Usually the pitch of the roof is such that the overhang can be extended 3' without getting low enough to interfere with head space. If there's any doubt whether the rafters can withstand the added load, get professional advice rather than risk damaging the roof.

One of the shade materials previously described is added to the top of the extensions. Lath or wood strips are the most logical choice since they tie in well with most house styles.

Window grilles are constructed by clasping the ends of the exposed rafter tails to form vertical posts. A 2"x4" return to the house wall at the bottom gives added support. Wood strips are nailed horizontally to the vertical posts as close or as far apart as you wish. Shade protection and view are prime considerations.

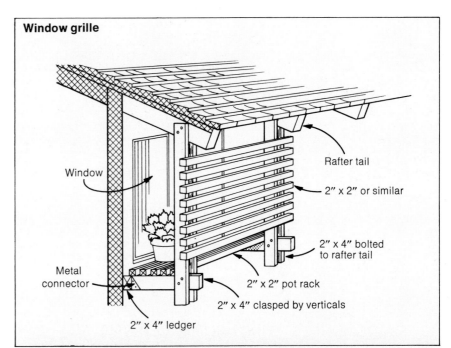

Window grille

Window

Metal connector

2" x 4" ledger

Rafter tail

2" x 2" or similar

2" x 4" bolted to rafter tail

2" x 2" pot rack

2" x 4" clasped by verticals

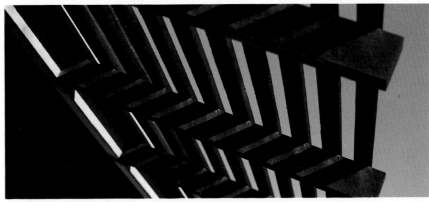

Roof line is extended by 2"x4"s bolted to house rafters with 1"x2"s on top. Fascia board was notched to receive added 2"x4"s.

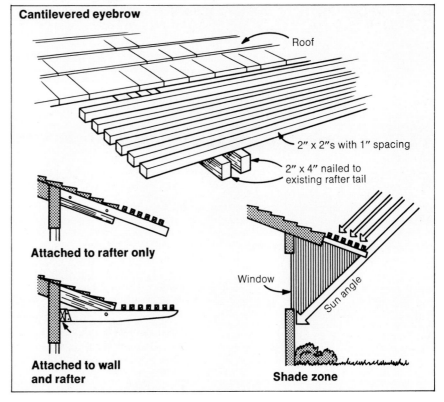

Cantilevered eyebrow

Roof

2" x 2"s with 1" spacing

2" x 4" nailed to existing rafter tail

Attached to rafter only

Attached to wall and rafter

Window

Sun angle

Shade zone

Storage sheds and work areas

There's no room for garden work or storage in this garage.

Metal storage sheds come in easy to assemble kits.

Gardening is a continuing process. It requires tools, equipment and materials, some of them bulky, smelly and potentially hazardous. Storage is a problem. The garage can serve, if it isn't already filled to overflowing with cars, bicycles, workshop tools, old furniture, trash cans, sports equipment and whatever else won't fit in the house. Additional space is almost always required.

Pre-fabricated storage sheds are available in a wide range of sizes and styles. They're easy to assemble, require no building permit, and are fireproof if constructed of metal. However, there are advantages in building a storage shed from scratch. It can be custom designed to fit the area and your specific needs; it can blend in with the house by using the same materials and colors; and you can save money and have fun by doing it yourself.

Using the house or the garage for the back wall is an economical way to construct a storage shed. Since the shed itself should be at least 3' wide, and another 3' or 4' is needed in front of it for access, the typical 5' side yard is inadequate. Unless you happen to have 10' or more to the property line, the back of the house or garage may be the only usable space. (Even then, check with the building department and read your deed restrictions before building.)

If there's an existing 3' or 4' roof overhang, all you need to do is add

◁

Top: A work center that responds to the seasons. In spring it is opened to provide entertainment area on patio side. Lower left: Opposite side is work and storage area. Lower right: In fall the extensions retract, the table folds away and the work center is dormant until spring again fills the air. Designer, John Matthias.

This storage gazebo is functional as well as attractive.

Convenient storage cabinet capitalizes on existing roof overhang.

Storage cabinet holds pots and hides meters.

side walls and doors on the front. Assuming this is almost too much to hope for, a new roof will also be required. In this case, it's not much more work or expense to make it at least 5' wide x 10' long, if there's room for it. Lay it out on the ground and proceed as follows:

1. Foundation — is normally 12" deep, 6" wide and 6" above grade, but in any case, should conform to local codes. Use 2"x6" form boards for poured concrete (see page 50), and set sill bolts 12" from the corners and 4' apart.

2. 2"x4" Ledger — should be attached to the wall with ½"x5½" lag bolts into every other stud. Determine how high it should be by taking the height of the door above the floor (normally 6'-8"), adding the depth of the beam and rafters above, and allowing a 4" per foot roof pitch. If the wall isn't high enough, consider a flatter roof, plywood instead of rafters, or lower doors.

3. Wall framing — is normally stud wall construction. Drill a 2"x4" sill (decay-resistant or treated), set it over the sill bolts and tighten-down with washers and nuts. Use 2"x4" studs

The owner built this simple storage-work shed in approximately 4 hours for a material cost of less than $50.00. The secret is in using the house wall as a back and a support.

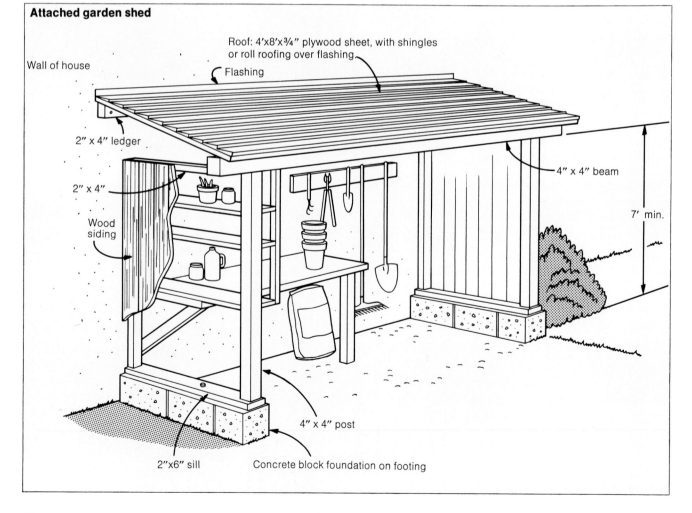

Attached garden shed

Roof: 4'x8'x¾" plywood sheet, with shingles or roll roofing over flashing

Wall of house

Flashing

2" x 4" ledger

2" x 4"

Wood siding

4" x 4" beam

7' min.

4" x 4" post

2"x6" sill

Concrete block foundation on footing

at 16" on center with a double 2"x4" top plate. A 4"x4" header is sufficient over a door up to 4' wide; increase to a 4"x6" for double 3' doors.

4. 2"x4" Rafters — spaced 16" on center are either set on top of the ledger or attached flush with metal connectors. Toenail the rafters to the top plate or header, after making sure the front wall is plumb. A minimum 12" overhang helps keep rain off the walls.

5. Sheathing — can be ½" exterior plywood or ¾" thick boards. Tongue and groove looks better and is stronger than plain boards.

6. Roofing — Ninety pound roll-type roofing with a mineral aggregate surface may be used when the roof pitch is less than 4" in 12". Roll it out on top of the sheathing, cut to size and nail into place. Use cold tar for overlaps and be sure overlaps occur from top to bottom. Roll roofing is inexpensive, lasts for 5 to 10 years under normal conditions, and new layers can easily be added.

Asphalt or wood shingles are better when the roof is visible, but should have a minimum slope of 4" in 12". Attach them with 4d shingle nails over a layer of 30 lb. roofing paper.

7. Flashing — must be installed at the intersection of wall and new roof unless the joint is adequately protected by an existing overhang. Metal flashing can be sealed directly against a smooth wall with mastic. Another way is to cut a notch ½" deep in the wall and imbed the flashing with mastic.

8. Wall covering — of wood siding is popular and looks especially good if it matches the house walls. Application is similar to fence construction except a layer of 30 lb. felt behind the siding is recommended to make it rain-proof.

9. Doors — are desirable for weather protection and security. They can be more like gates (see page 54) or you can use conventional house doors. Doors can be omitted if the weather is mild and security is not a goal.

10. Flooring — can be solid or soft paving as desired. If schedules permit, it's a good place to use surplus concrete from another pour.

A free-standing storage shed requires a back wall, of course. If there's enough room, you can consider expanding it to a 10'x10' building by using 2"x6" rafters. A window will provide light and ventilation.

Such structures provide a place to store garden paraphernalia, but can

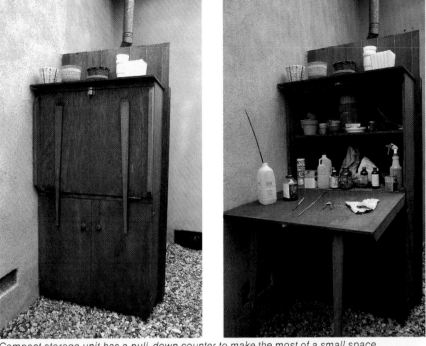

Compact storage unit has a pull-down counter to make the most of a small space.

Storage unit is being built into the fence to make use of a narrow side yard.

Completed project blends into fence.

also do for potting, propagating, fertilizer and insecticide mixing, repairing
and other gardening tasks.

A sturdy work bench which you can
build either inside or adjacent to
the shed serves well for such uses.
A 2″x4″ frame 36″ high and 24″ wide,
topped with 2″ lumber, provides a
surface wide enough to set pots and
tools on while working. The height
is good whether you are standing or
sitting on a long-legged stool. Fit storage containers for topsoil, peat moss,
fertilizers, and the like underneath, but
leave room to remove the lids. Determine bench-length to suit your needs,
then add a bit more. There never
seems to be enough bench space.

An old patio dining table is excellent
for garden work and has the advantage of being portable. Place it under
a tree in the summer, and move it
against a sunny wall to trap the heat
on chilly days.

A sink with cold water is valuable
for cleaning vegetables, arranging cut
flowers, mixing fertilizer and insecti-

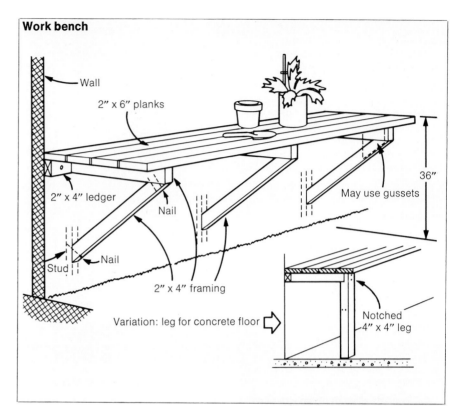

Work bench

Wall

2″ x 6″ planks

2″ x 4″ ledger

Nail

Stud

Nail

36″

May use gussets

2″ x 4″ framing

Variation: leg for concrete floor ⇨

Notched
4″ x 4″ leg

Free-standing storage shed uses doors for miscellaneous items.

*A work area can also be a pleasant place
to relax.*

*Storage and potting area is hidden on
other side of this display area.*

cides and washing pots, tools and hands. Building codes are strict, and usually require connection to a sanitary sewer or disposal system.

This may or may not be practical, depending upon the depth and location of the sewer pipe. In some well-drained soils, a dry well or leach field trench filled with crushed rock can handle the water, and may be allowed by local codes.

An extended roof — either solid or in the form of a shade structure—can make the area more comfortable for working. If you block the wind and provide enough room, it becomes a garden work center that will serve both people and plants.

Seedlings and cuttings can be started in such protected areas with greater success than when exposed to the elements. In such a nice atmosphere, you're more apt to give them necessary care. It's also a good place to establish a "hospital" for ailing plants and for storage of potted plants during winter months.

Lath overhead, storage bins and long work bench make this a comfortable and usable area.

A sink can extend the usefulness of a work area tremendously.

Poolside storage bench with lid closed is wide enough for sun-bathing.

Life jackets and pool toys are conveniently hidden from sight.

Weekend and in-between projects

One of the intriguing aspects of garden-building activities is that the range of projects is so diversified. Small projects you accomplish successfully can make you appreciate your potential to go on to larger ones.

The experienced amateur knows the value of doing a quickee project or two, between major ones. The change of pace is like a second wind and is especially appealing when the result is an accessory that makes the garden more attractive or more functional. Here then, are projects designed for doing over a weekend, or the span of a few evenings.

Do anticipate and provide for the materials you will need for the project. Don't wait for the workday to do this, since it can cut down on the time you have allotted for construction phases. It can be quite frustrating to have to stand in a waiting line at the store, when you are eager to get to the sawing, or digging, or whatever. Study the instructions for a particular project—think out the steps—do the project mentally. You will be impressed with how this will prepare you for the actual doing.

Benches

Many garden benches can be completed in a week-end and enjoyed immediately.

Wood is the most popular material for garden benches. They can be simple or elaborate with or without backs, or made in combination with other materials such as brick or block.

Storage bench

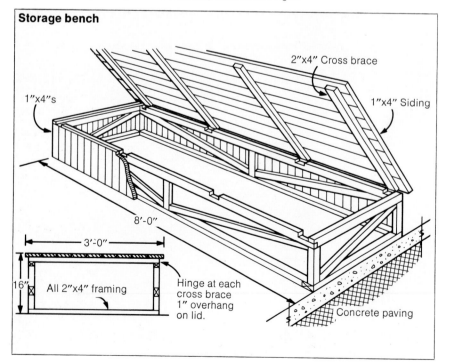

Two 4"x8" planks on wood, masonry or steel supports placed 6' apart, form a fine seat that is in scale with a large garden area. Nine or ten 2"x4"s placed on edge ¼" apart can span the same distance and do not look quite as heavy. Use 3 wood supports and five 2"x4"s laid flat as the seat, and you have a light-weight, portable bench.

Generally garden benches are slightly lower and broader than chairs. 16" high and about as wide is a good rule.

Widen a bench to 24" or more and you have a lounge or sun-bathing platform. Enclose the sides and hinge the top and you provide storage space for outdoor equipment. Use seasoned, surfaced lumber. Chamfer all edges and sand enough to eliminate slivers and splinters. A coat of polyurethane applied as needed will keep the surface smooth and easier to clean.

Curved benches are dramatic and feasible if you work with correct materials, or you can use straight segments with mitered joints to get the feeling of a curve.

You can work with most any material thickness (up to 1½") so long as the design-curve is reasonable. Naturally, ½" stock will bend more easily than heavier material and will turn a tighter corner. 1"x3" stock (net = ¾" x 2½") seems compatible for such projects and will bend adequately when used on edge and separated with ½" thick wood spacers. It makes sense to see how much you can bend a piece of wood before you design the project. Then you can choose a thickness that will work for you. Do select material that is free of knots since such areas can crack under bend-pressure. Assembling can be done with galvanized nails or screws or, for super security use a threaded rod that passes completely through the parts. The threaded rod, together with nuts and washers, is available in most large hardware stores.

Fire-pits

Fire-pits, like campfires, have universal appeal. The warmth of an open fire is a pleasant experience, and it can make a garden usable even when the weather is cool. A fire-pit is especially useful for garden parties since it's often the difference between staying outdoors, or having to retreat into the house.

Right: All wood construction of curved bench makes it easy to build without welding or special hardware. Landscape Architect, Chandler Fairbank.

Entire bench is made from 2"x4"s, with nailed connections throughout. See detail below.

This permanent bench has cross supports cut from 2" x 10"s bolted to square steel posts set in concrete. 2" x 3"s on end span 4' without sagging.

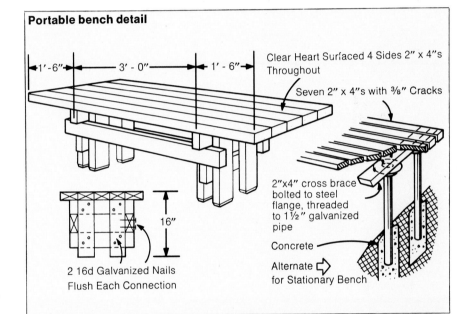

Portable bench detail

1'-6" 3'-0" 1'-6"

Clear Heart Surfaced 4 Sides 2" x 4"s Throughout

Seven 2" x 4"s with ⅜" Cracks

16"

2 16d Galvanized Nails Flush Each Connection

2"x4" cross brace bolted to steel flange, threaded to 1½" galvanized pipe

Concrete

Alternate ⇨ for Stationary Bench

Four separate benches are butted to form a wood deck for sitting and lounging.

Benches are moved back to reveal a wood-burning fire-pit with seating for 16 people.

Red volcanic rock harmonizes with curbing of half bricks. Portable benches allow swimmers to choose comfortable distance from fire.

There's no reason why a fire-pit can't be used to some extent for outdoor cooking. Polynesian type baking, or just burying of foil-wrapped meats, corn and potatoes in the coals is especially fun.

Since the basic function of a fire-pit is to provide warmth in a particular area, it may not be as convenient for serious cooking as a special built-in barbecue or one that you can wheel about. Often, its design puts the project's surface at ground level or thereabout which means a lot of uncomfortable squatting or stooping. So bear such thoughts in mind if cooking is a necessary factor. Try to choose the location that is best for double-duty use; one that is protected from the wind. An adjustable grill will do much to make the project more functional.

Check with your fire department to see if open wood fires are allowed before you start to build. Natural gas, when available, is cleaner, and easier to start than wood. Covering the gas flames with non-explosive volcanic rocks provides a radiant heat effect and a beautiful glow and the rocks are more ornamental than cold ashes.

Permanent seating limits choice of distance from the flames so it's a good idea to leave some room for movable furniture. Sinking the entire area and using the surrounding wall as a seat can be very effective, when the distance between wall and flames is planned for comfort.

A removable cover over a flush pit allows unobstructed patio space when the pit is not in use. A seat or table, made to fit over a raised fire-pit, is a good way to hide it while increasing function.

Simplest construction is a ring of rocks around a hole in the ground; charming if you have property that permits setting aside a special area. In most gardens, the best location is a convenient paved, outdoor living area, clear of tree branches or roof overhangs.

A low masonry wall lined with fire bricks will keep volcanic rock or ashes neatly in place. A 4' diameter or square is a good size. Install a valve outside the wall if natural gas is used. Most times, the gas is fed through a drilled pipe laid on a gravel base in the form of a cross 6″± below the top of the wall. A drain in the bottom of the pit makes sense. This can tie-in to

Brick fire-pit with curved seat was built by the owner with little previous bricklaying experience. Note slanted backrest and decorative tile.

Slump type concrete block set on end forms fire-pit circle. Inside is thick coat of mortar mixed with fire-clay.

Circular lid of 2" x 4"s sets flush with concrete paving to cover this sunken fire-pit when not in use. Lid removed to show fire brick lining and gas piping. Valve is close enough to permit lighting by one person.

Simple fire-pit of loose laid bricks can be easily relocated if desired.

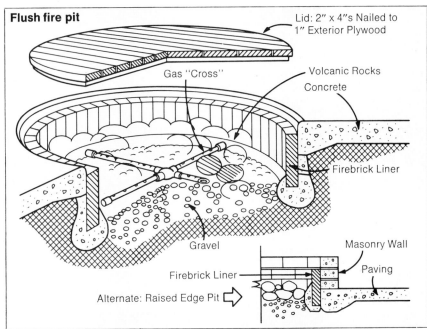

Flush fire pit

Lid: 2" x 4"s Nailed to 1" Exterior Plywood

Gas "Cross"

Volcanic Rocks

Concrete

Firebrick Liner

Gravel

Firebrick Liner

Masonry Wall

Paving

Alternate: Raised Edge Pit ➡

Brick mowing strip in front of brick planter makes lawn edging easier.

Concrete block planter has back wall to keep soil away from house wall. Metal flashing further protects house from moisture.

Masonry planter against a wall

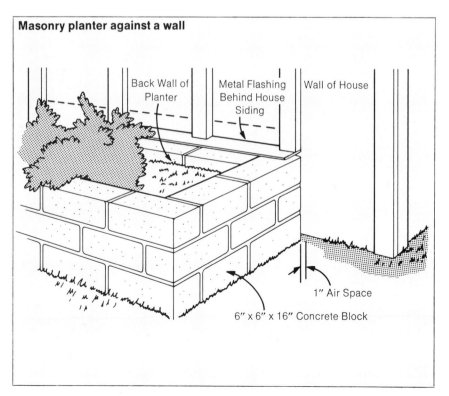

Back Wall of Planter

Metal Flashing Behind House Siding

Wall of House

1" Air Space

6" x 6" x 16" Concrete Block

an established drainage system. Another solution is to dig a 3' deep dry well underneath filled with crushed rock.

Raised planters

Raised planters or raised beds are a fine solution when you have poorly-drained, shallow soil, or wish to protect plants (especially prized specimens) from being trampled.

The project doesn't have to be more than curbing that defines the planting area and allows for additional topsoil. Railroad ties, pressure-treated timbers and telephone poles laid directly on the ground are a natural for this use, or you can work with concrete block, poured concrete, brick, broken concrete or stone.

Since a planter often functions as a retaining wall, it must be constructed to support the pressure of the fill. Consequently, cost increases along with wall height. Limiting the height to under 3' will avoid overly expensive construction. Since a wall in the area of 18" high can serve as a seat, it may pay to make it at least 12" wide even though the additional width is not required for strength.

Similar materials and construction techniques are applicable for both low and medium height planters. (See chapters, "Fences and Walls," and "Recycled and Inexpensive Materials"). As with any garden construction, try to select a material and color that either is the same, or compatible with the house.

Don't make the error of designing planters so they are too narrow or too shallow for the plants you have in mind. A little too large is better than too small. For example, there are few permanent shrubs that stay less than 24" wide for any length of time without considerable pruning. Large shrubs and small trees require widths up to 10 feet.

Don't build a planter and then use fill-soil directly against the wall of the house. Applying a bituminous sealer and crushed rock against the house wall is better than nothing at all, but it's a minimum effort and doesn't guarantee that moisture will not seep through. A back wall, separated from the house by an air space of several inches, is a better way to insure against leakage. Include weep holes in the wall to allow water to drain out away from the house.

Filling soil against the trunk of a tree can be almost as disastrous as filling against a house wall. Most trees are highly sensitive to changes in grade; building a planter around a

Planter gives this house a longer, lower appearance.

Raised concrete block planter accents entrance with brilliant display of annuals.

Benches or raised planters are pleasant around trees. One caution—do not use soil-fill around trunk as this may damage or even the kill the tree.

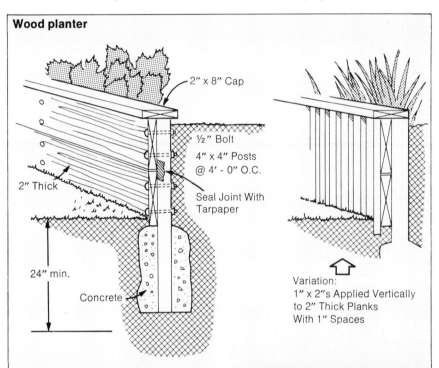

Wood planter

2" x 8" Cap

½" Bolt

4" x 4" Posts @ 4' - 0" O.C.

Seal Joint With Tarpaper

2" Thick

24" min.

Concrete

Variation: 1" x 2"s Applied Vertically to 2" Thick Planks With 1" Spaces

Redwood 2" x 12" plank planter allows for the addition of topsoil for back yard vegetable garden.

Bolted connections to 4" x 4" posts sunken 24" deep will keep planks from warping and pulling loose.

Cap on raised planter provides finished look and a place to sit when gardening.

Gently arching bridge is simple to construct using curved ribs cut from 2"x12"s.

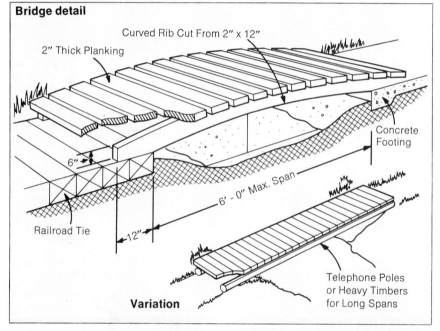

Bridge detail

2" Thick Planking

Curved Rib Cut From 2" x 12"

Concrete Footing

6"

6' - 0" Max. Span

12"

Railroad Tie

Telephone Poles or Heavy Timbers for Long Spans

Variation

tree may look good—until the tree dies. A safe way to achieve the same effect is to build the planter and not fill with soil, making sure water can easily get out. Then set plants in containers behind the wall rather than planting in the ground.

Bridges

Did you ever consider you can have a bridge even though you don't have to cross a river? Even the flimsiest excuse is justifiable; a bridge can add a romantic element to the garden that few other features can. Building a bridge is so fascinating that it's more recreation than work. Besides, drainage flow lines, dry stream beds and changes in levels often necessitate some means of getting across.

Designs can range from a single log laid over a rivulet, to an arching masterpiece reaching across a garden pond. Leaving the under-structure exposed to reveal construction techniques adds to the interest.

A suitable stone slab makes a nice natural bridge or you can do with a 6" thick, reinforced-concrete slab that you pre-cast and set in position, or pour on location.

Wood bridges are justifiably popular. If the soil is reasonably stable, you can avoid the chore of casting footings by resting railroad ties, treated timbers, or telephone poles directly on the ground. Railroad ties are limited to crossings of approximately 4' since you should allow 2' bearing on each end. Treated timbers are available in larger dimensions and longer lengths, but for spans of 10' and greater, telephone poles are ideal. Butted railroad ties and timbers can be walked on directly but telephone poles are best covered with 2" thick planks to provide a flat surface.

Piers or footings are necessary in soggy or unstable soil. Telephone poles can be installed vertically if holes are dug down to firm soil. Masonry footings must sit on firm soil and should be high enough to keep wood at least 6" off the ground. Plan the span so footings can be out of water.

For small bridges, railings can be omitted, or limited to a few guide posts. Larger bridges may require railings for safety. Allowing telephone-

Far left: Tiny stream bed runs under simple bridge, adding interest to this front entrance walk. Left: Bridge of peeled logs and rough planks seems just right for this natural setting.

pole piers to extend above the bridge provides posts for chain, rope, or wood railings. Attach conventional wood railings so they are sturdy—add bracing if necessary to prevent wobbling.

In general, basic deck and railing construction as described in "Garden Floors and Decks" can be applied to bridges.

Garden trellises

Espaliered plants and vines require a sturdy frame or trellis to grow on. Usually the structure is secondary to the plant growth although it can be the dominant element when the foliage is only a tracery.

2"x2" stock is a better basic size for this use rather than 1"x1". It's stronger and more in scale with garden proportions. It also holds the plant out farther when used against a wall, reducing reflected heat damage and allowing more air circulation behind.

2"x2"s can be lag-bolted directly to the wall. If you place them horizontally 12" apart you can use nails or wires wherever they might be needed. Vertical 2"x2"s placed 16" on center to hit studs, plus horizontal members, provides a ladder on which plants can be trained without ties. The 2"x2"s can be stained a contrasting color, or blended with the wall to be almost invisible.

Another way of building a trellis against a wall is to bolt uprights to the ends of protruding rafter tails. Two 2"x2"s at each rafter will look balanced. Horizontal cross pieces can be added if desired. An advantage of this method is that the wall is not touched by the trellis, and by loosening or removing the bolts, it can be tipped outwards or taken down to allow access for painting behind.

A trellis spanning an opening in a fence, or over a gate can be an attractive addition if it fits into your plan. Pre-fabricated units are often flimsy and underscaled so building one is the way to go if you wish the design to relate to your needs and desires.

This type of construction is almost like a miniature arbor or pergola. The difference is that you set the posts more closely together (a 3' x 4' retangle will do for a small gate), and you can sink them directly in the ground. Use 2" x 4" or 4" x 4"s for the frame; add 2" x 2"s on top and up the sides in the manner of a ladder, for plants to grow on. Stain or paint to relate to existing structure and motif.

Vertical 2"x2"s with horizontal 1"x1" form simple fence trellis.

Handsome walk-under trellis is especially dramatic because of its imposing height. Landscape Architect, Casey Kawamoto.

Trellis of 2"x2" hangs from roof fascia; serves three purposes — privacy, shade and plant support.

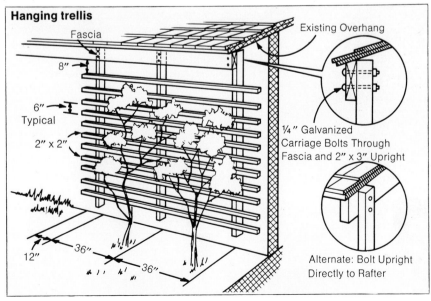

Hanging trellis

Fascia

Existing Overhang

8"

6" Typical

2" x 2"

¼" Galvanized Carriage Bolts Through Fascia and 2" x 3" Upright

12"   36"   36"

Alternate: Bolt Upright Directly to Rafter

Raw materials pictured above can be transformed by the imaginative garden builder: 1. Railroad ties 2. Broken concrete 3. Discarded tires

Recycled and relatively inexpensive materials

Everybody loves a bargain and it's always pleasant to find materials that cost less than expected. Garden building presents the opportunity to utilize certain premium quality materials that not only cost less than "brand new," but also impart a casual and comfortable effect. Since you're helping the environment by using things that might otherwise be burned or buried, you can feel good as you save money.

Prices do vary though; from "free for the hauling," to really no bargain at all. Today's interest in utilizing discarded items often causes prices to soar. So look around and compare. Classified ads in local newspapers and salvage companies are good sources. Sometimes you can put your name on a waiting list with a contractor or company that might come up with what you're looking for. Don't forget to include the rental cost of a truck or trailer, if you have to provide transportation, and don't have a large enough vehicle.

Almost any sturdy, weather-resistant material can be used for some type of garden construction if it suits the general motif. Some are recycled, some are salvaged, some are products of a manufacturing process.

Others are natural materials that can be gathered for the asking. Railroad ties, salvaged timbers, railroad-car stakes, broken concrete, used brick and telephone poles are among the most familiar recycled materials that appear in home gardens. Branches, canes, palm fronds and stalks are examples of natural materials that can sometimes be put to use rather than being hauled away.

Gathered and found materials

Imagination is the key word when it comes to using gathered and found materials, or objects, for garden building. Natural materials usually fit in better than discarded manufactured items, but it's surprising how you can dream up a super project with a reject scorned by others.

Look to other parts of the world to see some beautiful examples. Bamboo is used in the Orient as fencing, poles, trellises and the like. If you live outside the bamboo belt (some varieties actually survive snow), you can use poles made from tree prunings or thinned-out saplings in similar fashion.

Desert regions in the southwestern United States and Mexico exhibit

4. Wire cable spools 5. Telephone poles. 6. Used brick.

Recycled materials for garden construction

Name	Description and Comments	Cost Range
Railroad Ties	6"x8" rough timber, 8' long, usually pressure-treated with creosote. Condition of tie and type of lumber vary. Redwood is easiest to cut and work with. Excellent for curbing, low walls, steps.	$1.00 to $8.00 each
Treated Timbers	4"x4" and larger dimensions. Same uses as railroad ties, except better condition and choice of size.	$8.00 to $10.00 for size comparable to railroad tie.
Telephone Poles	8" to 24" diameter, pressure-treated poles. Lay horizontally as a curbing; vertically for low walls, barriers, posts.	$.50 to $2.00 per lineal foot
Car Stakes	3"x6"x9' long. Used under lumber loads on railroad flat cars. Being replaced with different methods, not as available as before. Good for rough types of above grade garden construction.	Often free to haul away, *when* available
Plywood Cores	5" diameter, flattened on 2 sides and pressure treated. Left over from peeling log in manufacture of plywood. Use for curbings, low walls, posts.	$4.00 to $5.00 for 8' length
Broken Concrete	A size approximating 4" thick x 12" wide x 24" long is best for most garden walls and paving.	Usually free for hauling cost
Used Bricks	Salvaged bricks with old mortar chipped off. Same uses as for new brick, but offers immediate "old" appearance.	5¢ to 15¢ apiece— cleaned
Tires, Bottles, etc.	Discarded manufactured items, sometimes usable as a garden building material. Takes ingenuity to look good.	Free
Gathered Stone	Various types of stone, usually cleared from farm lands, building sites and residential lots. Test for stability before using.	Usually free, if you pick it up
Driftwood, bamboo, fronds, stalks, etc.	All kinds of natural materials. Some have a limited permanence, and may be fragile. Gathering can be fun, but get permission from the owner.	Free, if you gather and haul

Tires are used as ready-made plant basins in this vegetable garden. They also make good planter curbings at the base of a slope.

Bamboo poles and palm fronds provide free building materials for this beautiful shade shelter.

Gathered stones laid rip-rap fashion protect this slope from erosion.

It's hard to recognize that this gate was made from an old wire cable spool.

fences made from cholla and ocotillo branches and yucca flower stalks. In lands like these where lumber is scarce, the use is both practical, appropriate, and imaginative.

Palm fronds serve as roofs and enclosures throughout the tropics. Tied to the top of a shade structure, they throw a light shade and permit air circulation. When they start to deteriorate, they're easily replaced.

The ocean supplies much driftwood in many areas. Such weathered pieces of wood can be very effective in garden construction.

Perhaps the greatest challenge and the most satisfaction lies in utilizing manufactured items that normally go to the dump. Automobile tires make good raised planters, and if partially sunken, clash least with surrounding soil. Vegetable growers will find they are ideal for tomatoes and hill-type plants like squash and melons.

Bottles laid flat in mortar can provide a translucent panel in a masonry wall and a hand-crafted touch. Be careful though to avoid a junk-collector's effect. Think in terms of using bottles that are similar in size and color.

Get permission before you collect materials on others' property. The owner may be delighted but he may have "use-ideas" of his own!

Salvaged redwood 4"x6"s are sunken and toe-nailed with 30d galvanized nails.

Railroad ties and timbers

Considering the many thousands of miles of railroad tracks in the United States, the number of ties that have been installed is almost beyond comprehension. As tracks were abandoned or repaired, the ties were often given away or sold at a nominal cost. At one time the supply exceeded the demand, but since the popularity of the tie as a garden material has increased, so has the cost. In most areas prices now range from a minimum of about $2.50 each and can go as high or higher than $8.00 each. Even at top prices, ties can still be a bargain and a valuable garden material, if they are *ideal* for a particular project.

Sometimes decay-resistant or pressure-treated timbers are used in a similar manner as ties where ties are too expensive, or not available at all. Salvaged plywood cores fall into this category. They are the core of the log that remains after peeling layers off for the manufacture of plywood. Flattened on two sides and pressure-treated, they can be used in contact with the ground. Being smaller and lighter weight than ties, they're easier to handle and have a more finished appearance.

The typical railroad tie is 6"x8" and can be oak, redwood, fir or almost

Laid along edge of driveway, railroad tie curbing keeps dirt off paving, isn't broken by errant tires.

Railroad-tie curbing becomes a design element in this landscape.

Railroad tie is bolted to concrete block wall as vertical accent.

3"x6" car stakes were obtained free from railroad siding, soaked in preservative and laid directly in ground on a sand base. Expected life: 5 to 10 years.

Chain saw is easiest way to cut through hard railroad ties.

2-man saw will do the job if only cutting a few ties.

Railroad tie or treated timber wall

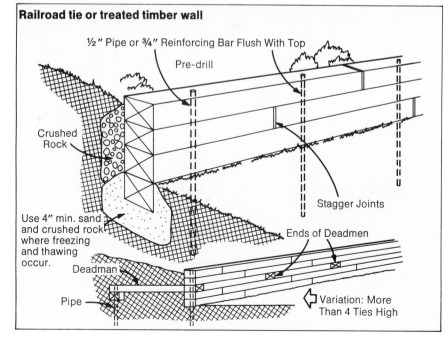

½″ Pipe or ¾″ Reinforcing Bar Flush With Top

Pre-drill

Crushed Rock

Use 4″ min. sand and crushed rock where freezing and thawing occur.

Deadman

Pipe

Stagger Joints

Ends of Deadmen

Variation: More Than 4 Ties High

any type wood. Full length is approximately 8′, but a new machine that runs on the tracks chops out the center section in 3′± lengths. This leaves ragged ends that need to be sawed-off for most uses.

In selecting ties, straightness and general appearance should be considered in relation to use; look for square edges for paving or steps. If the ties are used where they'll be exposed to hands, feet, clothing or plants, be sure to select the driest ones. Patches of wet creosote can be a real nuisance for both people and plants.

Outstanding characteristics of railroad ties are that they have a natural, rugged appearance, and can be used in direct contact with the ground. Their weight is another advantage, since they tend to hold position with a minimum of support.

It's a good idea to wear gloves when working with ties. They *are* heavy, so don't overdo when lifting, or get a helping hand. You sure don't want to drop one on a toe!

You can saw by hand but the job goes faster and better with a chain saw. Do watch for steel spikes that may have escaped removal.

Toe-nail with 30d spikes to secure one tie to another. For more security, in steps and walls for example, drill a 1″ diameter hole 12″ from the end and drive a ½″ pipe or ¾″ steel reinforcing rod into firm ground with a sledge hammer.

There are many uses for railroad ties in the garden. Three foot lengths are tailor-made for walks and paving. Set them at the toe of a slope as unobtrusive curbing or secure them with stakes or drilled pipes in the slope if you need to do terracing. They are great for step construction. The size and weight adapt beautifully to this use. (See chapter "Walks, Paths, Ramps and Steps," pages 28 to 33).

For retaining walls up to four ties high, pre-drill and overlap the ends so you can drive pipe or bar all the way through. Higher walls call for professional engineering. For a dramatic effect, dig a trench and place them vertically. This is okay for walls up to 3′ high if you sink them the same distance in the soil and never less than 24″. The tops can be level, or staggered at random.

Several other uses are: Place three or more side-by-side for a short bridge. Use as fence posts or bolt to a masonry wall as accent columns. Clean, dry ties can even be used as a seat or bench but be sure to sand them to eliminate slivers.

Heavy-duty drill is needed to drill most ties.

Steel pipe driven through drilled hole holds ties firmly in place.

Pipe should be driven slightly below surface of wood to avoid protruding sharp edges.

Leveling adjustments can be made by tapping steel pipe.

Ties are toe-nailed together with 30d nails for added strength.

Completed railroad tie planter will hold topsoil and protect planting.

Short pieces of telephone poles accentuate this stairway.

Low wall of random placed telephone-pole cross-sections is interesting backdrop for swimming pool.

Telephone pole deck post is extended as support for railing.

Pole sections, split in half, are used as curbing along sidewalk. Design, Dave Geller.

Shade structure is supported by sturdy telephone pole posts.

Beam is bolted to notched pole for strong and attractive connection.

Telephone poles

Like railroad ties, used telephone poles are great for garden construction. It takes a little imagination to look beyond the typical 50′ high tapering pole—scarred, weathered, and mottled with patches of black creosote—but treated poles are actually admirably suited to garden use. Their scale, texture and color blend well with plants and other garden materials, and the round shape is a pleasant contrast to more prevalent square and rectangular forms.

Finding the poles is part of the fun. Utility companies have widely different policies. Some gladly give old poles away for the hauling; others won't even consider it. Poles are often available from salvage companies and landscape-supply yards. Such places will charge more ($1.00 to $1.50 per lineal foot), but you can usually have them cut to length and delivered. Even at top prices, it's still a lot of lumber for the money.

Diameters of 10″ or 12″ are preferred for most landscape work, but diameters up to 24″ may be desirable for certain uses. Use relatively clean poles in good condition where they will be viewed at close range, or where splinters and creosote might create problems.

Working with poles is in many ways similar to railroad ties. Notching and bolting is the preferred method of connecting a flat piece of lumber to a round pole since the joint is very strong and looks good. Pole ends that are exposed to view should be chamfered (beveled) to improve appearance and eliminate splintering. This can be done with a sharp axe for a rustic effect, or with a hand or power saw for a smoother finish.

Poles are excellent for shade-structure posts, hillside deck supports, and similar post-type uses. Set on end in the ground side-by-side, they make a handsome retaining or free-standing wall. One pole laid horizontally, makes a good curbing, but for higher walls, the poles must be drilled and securely staked to keep them from rolling.

Large diameter poles can be used vertically as steps, with the cross-section serving as treads. They are often laid horizontally for step-ramps with soft paving or lawn for treads. However, the round face doesn't serve well as a riser for conventional steps.

Poles will span long distances and make great rustic bridges. Heavy planks laid on top provide a

Weathered character of these poles adds to effect in this casual grouping. Note chamfered tops.

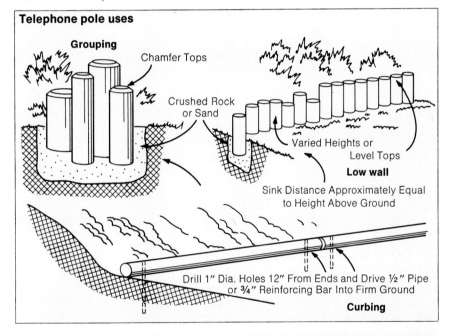

Telephone pole uses

Grouping

Chamfer Tops

Crushed Rock or Sand

Varied Heights or Level Tops

Low wall

Sink Distance Approximately Equal to Height Above Ground

Drill 1″ Dia. Holes 12″ From Ends and Drive ½″ Pipe or ¾″ Reinforcing Bar Into Firm Ground

Curbing

Pressure-treated plywood cores are used to face a low concrete block wall.

Peeled poles were soaked in preservative and installed at edge of stairs.

Planting softens dry wall of broken concrete.

Soil is used to level the courses of this broken concrete dry wall. Wall has considerable batter for stability.

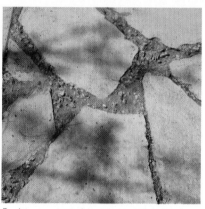

Broken concrete is an economical paving material. These pieces could be acid stained for a more stone-like effect.

Broken concrete wall

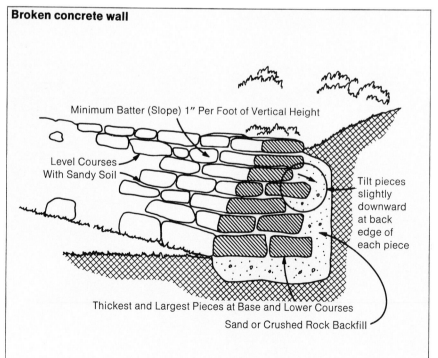

Minimum Batter (Slope) 1″ Per Foot of Vertical Height

Level Courses With Sandy Soil

Tilt pieces slightly downward at back edge of each piece

Thickest and Largest Pieces at Base and Lower Courses

Sand or Crushed Rock Backfill

safer walking surface than the rounded poles.

A very good ornamental use of poles is to sink them vertically at varying heights for use as pot display stands. By using different diameters, the effect is almost like a sculpture.

Broken concrete

If you can manage to be at the right place at the right time, and have a truck with you, broken concrete is one of the few materials that you can still get for free. The material is often misused but a well laid broken concrete wall can look good enough to stand on its own merits.

Walls can be laid dry, relying on gravity to hold them in place, or mortar joints can be used. The dry-wall technique is popular since spaces can be left for planting, and courses can be easily added or removed. Batter (slope) should be a minimum of 1″ per foot of vertical height.

The pieces will be easier to lay in courses if they don't vary more than ½″ in thickness. Pieces approximately 12″ wide x 24″ long are handy units to work with. Edges can be straightened and sizes modified with a heavy chisel and sledge hammer. Be sure to wear safety goggles! Footings are usually units of broken concrete set in the ground in a shallow trench. A 1″ to 2″ cushion of sand can be placed below the wall to make leveling easier. A poured concrete foundation with the first course imbedded while still wet, can also be used.

Broken concrete can also be used for garden paving. For this, the pieces of concrete can be more irregular

Used brick was selected to give this garden "instant age." Brick at pool edge is sealed to prevent flaking into the water.

Both paving and planter box are constructed of used brick. White on bricks ties in with house.

Square fire-pit, running bond paving and straight wall minimize brick cutting.

than for walls. Laying is similar to the various methods described for flagstones (see page 20). Utility areas and service walks are better choices for broken concrete paving, than for entry walks and outdoor living areas. Reason: even with excellent workmanship, it still ends up looking like broken concrete. Colored or salt-finish concrete is better than "plain old smooth gray."

Drainage swales (depressions) and gentle banks can be protected from erosion by laying broken concrete as a kind of rip-rap (irregular) paving. Turning the rough side up gives a more stone-like appearance.

Used brick

There was a time when used bricks sold for one cent each, all cleaned up and delivered to your door. They now are quickly sold at ten times the price, *when* you can find them. Popularity is one reason for the tremendous increase. The labor of chipping off the old mortar also adds greatly to the cost. If you get the bricks directly from a demolition site or salvage yard, and do the cleaning yourself, you can save some money. It takes time, but makes a great family project. Used bricks have essentially the same applications as new ones but do be aware that many building codes do not permit the use of used bricks in structural or load-bearing capacities. This is because the bricks may be so old they were not manufactured under quality-control conditions. Also, they may not bond securely when pores are filled with old mortar.

Used brick wall has entirely different feeling than if it were made of new bricks.

Rent a contractor's level to establish grades if drainage is critical. It can also be used to determine the height of posts, walls and other construction.

The narrow blade of a garden tractor is ideal for grading paths and is handy for moving soil in areas too small for larger equipment.

Hints, warnings and tips

Health and safety

Eight hours of work in the hot sun is a lot for anyone but can be especially fatiguing for the week-end contractor. Hands unaccustomed to working with shovels and heavy hammers can blister; seldom-used muscles can ache when tested. Garden-construction work can be done safely if all precautions are taken and you use good common sense. Don't take on more than you can handle.

All electrical tools MUST be properly grounded; double-insulated tools are preferable. Always use heavy-duty extension cords with a grounded connection. Respect all power tools, and wear safety goggles whenever there's a chance of flying particles. Read the manufacturer's instructions to be sure tools are properly adjusted. Sharp tools do a faster, safer and better job. Use the correct tool. Trying to drive a tack with a large claw hammer is an extreme example but illustrates what can lead to accidents. Borrow or rent instead of improvising with the wrong tool.

Lift properly with the legs rather than the back, and get help when the item is too heavy. Never try to do a two-person task by yourself.

Don't use rickety ladders or place yourself in a hazardous position on even a stable one.

It makes sense to have a comfortable work uniform that includes heavy, ankle-high shoes, preferably with a safety toe. Loose clothing is out. Keep sleeves buttoned tightly at the wrist or rolled well above your elbows. Wearing heavy gloves, when necessary, doesn't mark you as an amateur. Wear a hat (hard hats are available) if too much sun will bother you. Don't carry sharp tools in your pockets. Don't socialize while you work. If ever you are in doubt about the safety of a procedure, pause and consider . . . thinking twice is better than being hurt once. Don't ever become so over-confident that you become careless. Hang on to the beginner's respect and fear of tools—it's a great safety factor.

Footings and paving edges can be cut to exact shape with a straight spade.

Stubborn rocks can be pried loose with a heavy steel digging bar.

With a clam-shell digger it's easy to lift the soil out of a post hole.

A post hole can be drilled in seconds with a 2-man auger. It's worth the rental cost when quite a few holes are involved.

Electric jackhammer slices through hard and rocky soil. Requires only a 110 volt connection.

Install a carborundum blade and the versatile portable circular saw can be used to cut masonry.

Tools and equipment

Normal household tools will take care of many garden building needs. Check the sketches in the book for what tools are needed for a specific project. Then buy, borrow, or rent as needed to supplement what you already have. Rent expensive tools or pieces of equipment you may only use once or twice. Basic tools are best to own and will pay for themselves in a relatively short time.

Here is a list of tools and equipment that are helpful for garden building projects.

✓A sledge hammer or a smaller hand sledge for driving stakes, breaking rocks and similar jobs.

✓A small nail puller plus a wrecking bar for removing nails and prying.

✓A contractor's wheelbarrow for heavy loads and for mixing mortar and concrete.

✓A 7″ portable circular saw for cutting lumber. Usually the saw is equipped with a combination blade that is good for both ripping and cross-cutting, but you can substitute a rip blade, a crosscut blade, or even a special masonry blade.

✓A saber saw or a bayonet saw can make many useful cuts in the field. Either can be equipped with a special blade that will cut through an occasional nail.

✓Saw-horses can serve as workbenches or supports for scaffolding. Metal brackets that are used with standard 2″ x 4″s are available so you can assemble several units quickly.

✓A ⅜″ variable speed drill can be a great help. By using it with spade bits or hole saws you can drill holes up to 2½″ in diameter. Use it at low speed with tungsten-carbide bits to form holes in masonry.

✓A straight-edge spade is fine for cutting edges of footings and pavment forms.

✓A heavy steel digging bar is great for breaking through rocky soils other tools can't handle. Specialized pieces of equipment can be rented. Included are items like electric powered jack hammers (no compressor needed), powered post hole diggers, large heavy-duty portable drills, mixing machines for concrete, roto-tillers, small compactors and dozers, tamping and finishing machines for concrete, and the like.

Make judgements here in relation to the amount of work you must do. For example—don't attempt to do 50 or 60 post holes with a hand auger. Renting a power one increases the project cost, but it's worth it when you consider the time and energy you save. The cut-off point between working with a hand tool or a rented power tool is an arbitrary one. If you have but twelve holes to do and the power tool appeals, by all means go get one. Be sure you get adequate instructions for any tool you rent before you take it home.

Lumber yards are both fascinating and bewildering. Looking over the stock carefully and comparing prices can save a great deal of money.

Lumber

Don't be confused by the vast array of lumber on display in a local yard. Once you have decided size requirements you can choose grade and species to suit the job and your pocketbook. Quite often, an economical type will do, and may even look more appropriate. The salesman may be able to supply some good advice, yet it's a good idea to know something about the subject beforehand.

Size — The scale of the outdoors calls for larger members than are dictated by engineering requirements. Rafters, beams and posts in particular, should not look skimpy. When in doubt, consider the next largest size. It may be a better choice.

Species — Most wood used for garden construction is from conifers—softwood species. Douglas fir, larch, pine, cedar, cypress, redwood, spruce and hemlock are used in various parts of the country. Since many garden structures are oversized for appearance, comparative structural strength is not as important a factor as it is in house building. A redwood 4″ x 6″ rafter may not be as strong as one of douglas fir, but it will span 10′ just as well. However, since redwood costs more, choosing Douglas fir, or some other species, may be the wise economical move. Stain provides desired color.

Wood in contact with the ground (or concrete footings) should always be heartwood of a decay-resistant species such as redwood, cedar or cypress, or be pressure-treated.

Grade — Few garden projects require "Grade A," "Clear," or "Finish" lumber. Be careful with "Standard," or "Utility'" grades since they may be unsatisfactory. "#1 Common—Exposed" or "Construction—Exposed" applies to many species and is usually adequate for general garden requirements. Solid knots and minor surface defects are allowed in construction grades. The term "Exposed" means that for a slight increase in cost you can choose from the stack for appearance and straightness. Don't rely entirely on grade designations— make your own comparisons.

Dryness — Kiln-dried lumber always costs more and may not be available in the species you seek. "Seasoned" lumber is reasonably dry and will shrink a minimum amount. Avoid unseasoned lumber that is heavy because it contains an excess of water. Some may squirt at you when you nail.

Lengths — Lumber-lengths increase in multiples of 2', and 16' to 20' are the maximum lengths available in most yards. Some cutting-waste is unavoidable but you can minimize loss by making lists carefully, and by considering dimensional changes where necessary to adapt to available lengths. A deck that is 6½' wide results in cut-off waste whether you work with 8' or 14' lengths; 7' or 8' wide are better dimensions.

Surface—A rough or resawn finish may be preferable to surfaced-four-sides (s4s) material for many projects. Resawn surfaces are okay for decks, wood paving, and steps, but seats, railings, posts and vertical surfaces should be finished.

Grain and hardness — Wood surfaces that are subject to considerable foot traffic, such as steps or a deck, will wear down faster if made of redwood or cedar than if of a harder species. A soft wood is also more easily marked and scratched, but usually weathers better (lumber pressure-treated with "wolman" salts also weathers well). Douglas fir has a harder surface, but should be "vertical grain" to avoid long splinters. Except for extreme wear situations, it's somewhat of a toss-up as to which to use.

Lumber pricing — Most do-it-yourself lumber yards show lumber prices by the lineal foot even though the basic calculation relates to a board foot. Some yards, especially those catering to contractors state prices in terms of so much per thousand board feet. Either way, it's not a problem to compute costs whether you are talking lineal feet or board feet.

A board foot indicates a piece of wood that was originally 1"x12"x12". When you get it it will actually measure ¾"x11½"x12" but it will still be called a board foot. A 2"x12"x12" = 2 board feet as does a 1"x12"x24".

The formula for figuring board feet is to multiply length in feet by thickness in inches and width in inches and dividing by 12. Example: a 2"x8", 10' long = 10x2x8 = 160 ÷ 12 = 13⅓ board feet.

Plywood — Exterior grade plywood is a good material for fencing, gates, storage-building walls, roof sheathing and the like. Resawn or textured finishes are great. Siding types sold as "303 Exterior Siding—Group 4," or "303 Exterior Siding T1-11— Group 1," are types to consider. Redwood-veneered plywood weathers beautifully. Many times it is allowed to weather to a point and then sealed. All plywoods may be clear-sealed for a natural finish or stained or painted.

Textured plywood siding looks at home in the garden, and doesn't show minor flaws and scratches. Vertical ship-lap joint at left is almost invisible.

The chompings of carpenter bee larvae in this pecky cypress can be considered an asset.

Sound knots don't seriously affect the strength or beauty of lumber in most garden uses.

Close-up of rough-sawn board shows texture created by the saw blade at the lumber mill.

Nails, fasteners and glues

Nails are popular in garden building, but they should be rust-resistant. Galvanized nails are common but they do tend to rust at the heads, and can cause streaks on light colored wood. Stainless steel and aluminum nails cost slightly more (aluminum nails also bend more easily), but are preferred where even small rust marks are undesirable.

Wood should be securely fastened outdoors but using more and bigger nails is not the way to go. The correct size and number is always best. Generally, the nail should be 2½ to 3 times as long as the thickness of the board being secured. Thus, a 1"x4" (¾" net thick) can be attached with 6d or 8d nails; a 2"x4" (1½" net thick) requires at least a 16d nail. Nails with rings or threads on the shanks have extra holding power in all situations.

Use box nails when splitting is a problem, as they are thinner than common nails. Splitting can be minimized by providing as much distance from the edge as possible, and by blunting the tip of the nail with the hammer. Pilot holes slightly smaller than the nail diameter, can be pre-drilled in critical areas. Holding power may be reduced, so use a longer or threaded nail if possible.

The more nails driven into a piece of wood, especially if they are in line, the more chance there is of splitting. Two or three nails are usually used for pieces up to 8" wide. 10" and 12" boards may require three or four nails to prevent the center from warping. Nails driven at a slight angle hold better than nails driven straight.

You can hide nails when a fine finish is important but the job calls for driving the nails through counter-bored holes which are then plugged with a wooden peg. Finishing nails can be set below the surface of the wood—even box or common nails if you use a flat-face punch —and the resultant hole filled with a commercial wood dough or putty. This is a calculated risk though since many such products don't hold up well outdoors and they are difficult to color-match.

Driving the nail flush with the wood surface is okay for most jobs especially if you follow a neat pattern. If you drive the nail to within ⅛" of the surface and finish up by using a nail set for finishing nails or a punch for headed nails, you will avoid the possibility of marring the wood with hammer marks.

Two other nails commonly used in garden construction are:

Scaffold or double-headed nails (often called "duplex") are handy for temporary form work or braces. They also work well as places to secure strings or wires.

Masonry (case hardened) nails are extra strong, thick nails you can drive into most concrete and masonry surfaces. They work best in strong mortar joints but may require pilot holes in extra-hard surfaces and in materials that might split. Use a small hand sledge to drive them and always wear safety goggles.

Screws may be used when the joint may be disassembled later on, or where an extra strong joint is needed, or where there is little nailing depth. (Screws are best for gates). Installing a few screws is no problem, but a structure that requires a hundred entails much more work than nailing. Power drills (some require a special attachment) are now made for driving screws making the job much easier.

Flat-headed, or lag screws with a square or hex bolt-type head are usually preferred when the screw will be visible. (They can also be counter-sunk and pegged). The screw should penetrate at least ½ its length, or slightly less than the total thickness of the boards to be joined. A guide hole can be made with a punch or nail for small screws in soft woods, but use a drill for large holes and for hard woods. Small gauge screws that are long enough for the job are less apt to split the wood. For example, if you

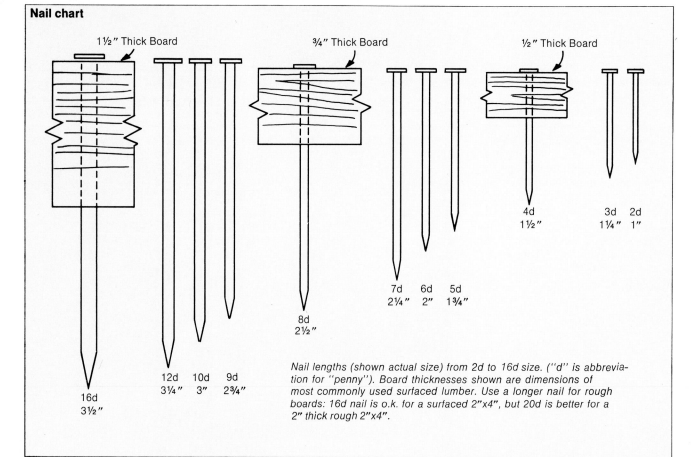

Nail chart

1½" Thick Board   ¾" Thick Board   ½" Thick Board

16d
3½"

12d   10d   9d
3¼"   3"   2¾"

8d
2½"

7d   6d   5d
2¼"   2"   1¾"

4d
1½"

3d   2d
1¼"   1"

Nail lengths (shown actual size) from 2d to 16d size. ("d" is abbreviation for "penny"). Board thicknesses shown are dimensions of most commonly used surfaced lumber. Use a longer nail for rough boards: 16d nail is o.k. for a surfaced 2"x4", but 20d is better for a 2" thick rough 2"x4".

need a 2″ long screw, an 8 or 9 gauge might be better than a 16 gauge. Coarse threads hold better in most garden wood. For heavy-duty connections, use lag screws and washers (often called lag bolts).

Bolts are real work-horses and should be used whenever nails, screws, or lags are inadequate. Carriage bolts are a good choice. They have a shoulder on the head side that grips the wood so the bolt can't turn when the nut is tightened. Always use a washer under the nut. ¼″ diameters for 1½″ thick lumber and ½″ diameters for 3½″ thick lumber are good choices. Allow ½″ extra length for the washer and nut, and use two bolts for load-bearing connections. Cadmium-plated bolts are best for outdoor work because of their rust resistance.

Expansion shields (of various materials) are used for attachments to masonry. Drill the correct-size hole with a masonry bit, or star drill, and press in the shield. The shield expands to grip the sides of the hole when you tighten the bolt or screw.

Metal connectors are easy to install and do a better job than nailing in certain cases. Post anchors are used to hold posts to slabs or footings; post caps serve in similar fashion to attach posts to beams. Joist hangers permit flush connections of rafters to beams, or ledgers. Angles, framing anchors and metal clips are available in many shapes and sizes and are fine to use where nailing is difficult, or extra strength is needed. Some connectors like joist hangers, require special nails, but you can check this out at the point of supply.

All metal connectors should be galvanized. If attached neatly and painted to blend, they're seldom objectionable in appearance.

Glues and adhesives often solve unique bonding problems. Type of glue, materials involved, mixing, application, and setting time, affect the strength of the joint. They are not used for structural connections where failure would be dangerous.

Resorcinol or epoxy resin glue can be used where nail heads are sometimes objectionable, such as a bench surface, especially as a supplement to finish nails that might not hold by themselves. Mastic, especially made for outdoor use, will hold wood directly on top of existing concrete and eliminate the need to install nailing members. Masonry units subject to loosening can be secured with concrete glue, either mixed in the mortar, or brushed on, to replace a dislodged piece.

Even galvanized nails can leave rust streaks. To avoid this use aluminum or stainless steel nails.

Cadmium-plated carriage bolts seat into the wood for a strong and unobtrusive connection.

Masonry bit is used to drill into concrete block and similar materials.

Expansion shield receives lag screw, can be used to hold boards, steel angles, cables, etc.

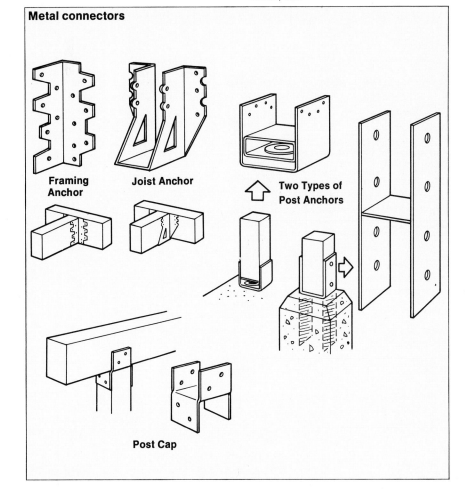

Metal connectors

Framing Anchor

Joist Anchor

Two Types of Post Anchors

Post Cap

Resource information

Watching, or working with a craftsman is the best way to learn how to build something. But we can't all be apprentices, or even be fortunate enough to find someone to watch. Generally an experienced person at a lumber yard or building supply company will be knowledgeable about the material, and also how to build with it. Large companies might also have some displays showing how the finished results should look. Friends and neighbors who have already attempted the project you are contemplating, are usually more than willing to offer advice. They might even lend a hand, or at least some tools.

In addition to personal help, there are many publications that are concerned with construction related to the garden. Some offer considerable detail on how-to-do-it, and may even include complete plans and specifications. The following organizations have some excellent books and pamphlets available at nominal cost.

American Plywood Association
1119 A Street
Tacoma, WA 98401
1. Catalog of Handy Plans
2. A Sampling of Plywood for Paneling and Siding
3. Finishing Plywood for Exterior Exposure

The Asphalt Institute
Asphalt Institute Building
College Park, MD 20740
1. Full-Depth Asphalt Pavements for Asphalt Driveways. CL-11
2. Model Specifications for Small Pacing Jobs. CL-2
3. Full-Depth Asphalt Tennis Courts. CL-4

Brick Institute of America
1750 Old Meadow Road
McLean, VA 22101
1. 16 Outdoor Brick Projects You Can Build. 50¢

California Redwood Association
617 Montgomery Street
San Francisco, CA 94111
1. Redwood Landscape Guide
2. Redwood Decks
3. Redwood Fences
4. Redwood Garden Shelters
5. Building a Redwood Garden Shelter. 3C2-3
6. Redwood Garden Work Centers. 3C2-4
7. Redwood Deck Construction. 3C2-5
8. Redwood Garden Retaining Walls. 3C4-1
9. Patio Paving With Redwood. 3C5-1

Goldblatt
Kansas City, KS 66110
Catalog of tools

Kraftile Company
800 Kraftile Road
P.O. Box 2907
Fremont, CA 94536
Booklet on "Laying Patio Tile"

Marshalltown Trowel Company
P.O. Box 738
Marshalltown, IA 50158
Booklet on "Troweling Tips and Techniques"

Portland Cement Association
Old Orchard Road
Skokie, IL 60076
1. Cement Mason's Guide to Building Concrete Walks, Drives, Patios and Steps. PA122H $2.50.
2. Concrete Improvements Around the House. PA003H $1.50.
3. How to Build a Patio of Ready-Mixed Concrete. IS094H 15¢.
4. Grounds for Good Living. PL001H $1.25.

Western Wood Products Association
1500 Yeon Building
Portland, OR 97204
1. Ideas for the Home Craftsman (list of plans and publications)
2. Western Wood Decks. 25¢
3. Three Do-It-Yourself Wood Decks. 25¢
4. Western Wood Fences. 25¢
5. 3 Fences of Western Wood. 25¢
6. Great Ideas in Outdoor Living. 25¢
7. Garden Tool House Plan #6. 25¢

Books

Concrete and Masonry—Design and Techniques
Reston Publishing Company

De Cristoforo's Complete Book of Power Tools
Popular Science Publishing Company

Concrete and Masonry—Design and Handbook
Arco Publishing Company

How-To Book of Concrete and Masonry
Fawcett Publications

Cooperative extension service

As the name implies, the Cooperative Extension Service is a *cooperative* effort of the United States Department of Agriculture and each state university.

There are 3,150 Extension Service Offices across the country—one in practically every county. One of the aims of the County Extension Agent is to put up-to-date information in the hands of the home gardener, but *you* have to ask for it.

Unfortunately there isn't a standardized name for the "County Agent" or the "Cooperative Extension Service" used consistently throughout the states. If you don't know who your County Agent is, the key is to look in the phone book under the name of your county for the Cooperative Extension Service, or to check in the yellow pages under the County Government Offices. If all else fails, you can write to your state university and request a list of County Extension Offices; they'll be happy to furnish the information.

Not only the county office but the university can be an invaluable source of information on many subjects. Below, we have listed the addresses of the state universities in your area. A letter to the office indicated of your state university, asking for a list of all available publications may bring you a surprising long list of bulletins, pamphlets and books.

State Extension Service offices

AK: Coop. Ext. Svc., *Univ. of Alaska,* College AK 99701.
AL: Coop. Ext. Svc., *Auburn Univ.,* Auburn AL 38630.
AR: Coop. Ext. Svc., *Univ. of Arkansas,* Box 391, Little Rock AR 72203.
AZ: Coop. Ext. Svc., *Univ. of Arizona* Tucson, AZ 85721.
CA: Public Service, University Hall, *Univ. of California,* Berkeley CA 94720.
CO: Bulletin Rm., *Colorado State Univ.,* Fort Collins CO 80521.
CT: Agricultural Publications, *Univ. of Connecticut,* Storrs CT 06268.
DE: Mailing Rm., Agricultural Hall, *Univ. of Delaware,* Newark DE 19711.
FL: Bulletin Rm., Bldg. 440, *Univ. of Florida,* Gainesville FL 32601.
GA: Coop. Ext. Svc., *Univ. of Georgia* Athens GA 30601.
HI: Publications Distribution Office, Krauss Hall, *Univ. of Hawaii,* 2500 Dole St., Honolulu HI 96822.
IA: Publications Distribution Center, Printing and Publications Bldg., *Iowa State Univ.,* Ames IA 50010.
ID: Mailing Rm., Agricultural Science Bldg., *Univ. of Idaho,* Moscow ID 83843.
IL: Agricultural Publications Office, 123 Mumford Hall, *Univ. of Illinois,* Urbana IL 61801.
IN: Mailing Rm., Agricultural Admin. Bldg., *Purdue Univ.,* West Lafayette IN 47907.
KS: Distribution Centre, Umberger Hall, *Kansas State Univ.,* Manhattan KS 66502.
KY: Bulletin Rm., Experiment Station Bldg., *Univ. of Kentucky,* Lexington KY 40506.
LA: Publications Librarian, Rm. 192, Knapp Hall, *Louisiana State Univ.,* Baton Rouge LA 70803.
MA: Coop. Ext. Svc., Stockbridge Hall, *Univ. of Massachusetts,* Amherst MA 01002.
MD: Agricultural Duplicating Services, *Univ. of Maryland,* College Park MD 20742.
ME: Dept. of Public Information, PICS Bldg., *Univ. of Maine,* Orono ME 04473.
MI: MSU Bulletin Office, Box 231, *Michigan State Univ.,* East Lansing MI 48823.

MN: Bulletin Rm., Coffey Hall, *Univ. of Minnesota.* St. Paul MN 55101.
MO: Publications, B-9 Whitten Hall, *Univ. of Missouri,* Columbia MO 95201.
MS: Coop. Ext. Svc., *Mississippi State Univ.,* State College MS 39762.
MT: Extension Mailing Rm., *Montana State Univ.,* Bozeman MT 59715.
NB: Dept. of Information, Col. of Agriculture, *Univ. of Nebraska,* Lincoln NB 68503.
NC: Publications Office, Dept. of Agricultural Info., Box 5037, *North Carolina State Univ.,* State College Station, Raleigh NC 27607.
ND: Dept. of Agricultural Information, *North Dakota State Univ.,* Fargo ND 51802.
NH: Mail Svc., Hewitt Hall, *Univ. of New Hampshire,* Durham NH 03824.
NJ: Bulletin Clerk, Col. of Agriculture, *Rutgers Univ.,* New Brunswick NJ 08903.
NM: Bulletin Office, Dept. of Agricultural Info., Drawer 3A1, *New Mexico State Univ.,* Las Cruces NM 88001.
NV: Agricultural Communications, *Univ. of Nevada,* Reno NV 89507.
NY: Mailing Rm., Bldg. 7, Research Park, *Cornell Univ.,* Ithaca NY 14850.
OH: Extension Office, *Ohio State Univ.,* 2120 Fyffe Rd., Columbus OH 43210.
OK: Central Mailing Services, *Oklahoma State Univ.,* Stillwater OK 74074.
OR: Bulletin Mailing Service, Industrial Bldg., *Oregon State Univ.,* Corvallis OR 97331.
PA: Sales Supervisor, 230 Ag. Admin. Bldg., *Pennsylvania State Univ.,* University Park PA 16802.
RI: Resource Information Office, 16 Woodward Hall, *Univ. of Rhode Island,* Kingston RI 02881.
SC: Dept. of Agricultural Communications, 112 Plant and Animal Science Bldg., *Clemson Univ.,* Clemson SC 29631.
SD: Agricultural Information Office, Extension Bldg., *South Dakota State Univ.,* Brookings SD 57006.
TN: Agricultural Ext. Svc., *Univ. of Tennessee,* Box 1071, Knoxville TN 37901.
TX: Dept. of Agricultural Communications, *Texas A&M Univ.,* College Station TX 77843.
UT: Ext. Publications Officer, Library 124, *Utah State Univ.,* Logan UT 84321.
VA: Ext. Division, *Virginia Polytechnic Institute,* Blacksburg VA 24061.
VT: Publications Office, Morrill Hall, *Univ. of Vermont,* Burlington VT 05401.
WA: Coop. Ext., Publications Bldg., *Washington State Univ.,* Pullman WA 99163.
WI: Agricultural Bulletin Bldg., 1535 Observatory Dr., *Univ. of Wisconsin,* Madison WI 53706.
WV: Coop. Ext. Svc., *West Virginia Univ.,* Morgantown WV 26506.
WY: Bulletin Rm., Col. of Agriculture, *Univ. of Wyoming,* Box 3354, Univ. Station, Laramie WY 82070.

Landscape architects
These highly trained specialists can help solve your problems in landscape design and construction. Check the yellow page listings for your area to locate landscape architects or write to:

American Society of Landscape Architects
1750 Old Meadow Road
McLean, VA 22101

American Institute of Landscape Architects
501 E. San Juan
Phoenix, AZ 85012